EVERYBODY'S DOING IT

Advertising Redefined
by an SEO Expert

I0464113

KELLEN KAUTZMAN

Everybody's Doing It
Advertising Redefined by an SEO Expert

Table of Contents

Page

Dedication

To Mom & Dad, we miss you.

ACKNOWLEDGMENTS

Lonaeja, thank you for your continued love and support during the countless nights required to make this book a reality.

A huge thank you to Kevin Kautzman for lending your impeccable editing skills to this project. This book would not be what it is today without your help.

Bree, there is no way I could have written this without your unbelievable talent and ability to manage Send It Rising so well.

Lisa, thank you for your support and honest feedback.

To all my friends and family that have supported me over the years, Dale, Levi, Chelsey, Todd, Han, Aaron, Lisa, Dr. Boyd, Chris, Shamika, Ian, Duane, Crystal, Andy, Melissa, Doug, Reannon, Sheryl, Matt, Alex, Cassidy, Clint, Phillip, Ryan, Bill, Joan, Joel, Robert, Kristi, Ali, Jen, Mark, Megan, Dario, Kirk, Destiny, Emily, Luis, Wendy, Eric, Chad, Reed, Susan, Sam, Charles and Dave.

INTRODUCTION

"Advertising is Not a Dirty Word"

People of the world! The Internet presents boundless opportunity for business. I know firsthand, having come of age at the dawn of widespread Internet. I've worked in digital marketing for a decade and have helped clients, from the local plumber to celebrities, achieve success online.

I wrote this book for anyone who has ever felt their business could be doing more online with digital marketing, but don't know where to start. Within, you will find my ideas on the essence of contemporary advertising, as well as universal principles I've identified that will remain relevant even as trends and technologies change. Often, I relate specific cases relevant to contemporary digital advertising back to universal principles, in order to demonstrate both current best practices and the guidelines that remain constant while the media changes.

Why do I insist on the word "advertising" when advertising online is now typically called "digital and/or Internet marketing?" Those terms certainly seem to appeal more to current sensibilities. The word "advertising" provokes for many images of Madison Avenue shenanigans, used car salesmen, and morally dubious cigarette commercials. So, I use "advertising" in order to be clear, and to make a statement:

Advertising is not a dirty word.

We should embrace advertising. Advertising is only the desire to gain and maintain attention. If you believe in your product or service, you should be proud to bring it to market, and advertising is how it's done, whatever you call it. The fundamentals of the game haven't changed, from printed media through to the Internet. To advertise successfully we need to go to where the people are, earn and hold their attention, relate with them, form a bond, and ask for their business.

Whether you are fighting to grow your business or strengthen existing relationships, advertising is key. No business exists that is not dependent upon its ability to earn and maintain attention.

Now, why should you listen to me?

In 2005 I set the goal to achieve 1,000,000 views online. I achieved that goal in 2010, by which point I knew that advertising online was my passion. In my work as a professional blogger, the Director of Operations for ADvise Media Group and now as the owner of Send It Rising Internet Marketing, I've managed campaigns for hundreds of clients from hotels on the Las Vegas Strip to doctors, accountants and celebrities you'd recognize. Send It Rising currently manages $76,000 a month in pay per click ads.

I've seen clients get to position one in Google for the most relevant and highly searched terms in their industry. Their entire livelihood pivots around this new attention. New homes are purchased and employees hired.

My clients have called me to express their gratitude for the work we've done, telling me that their phone rings all day long. I've heard phrases such as, "We've hired countless companies like yours, and I've never seen results like this."

The reason our clients succeed where others fail is that we work not only for, but with them. We coach our clients to do the things no digital marketing company can do on their behalf. And that's key for the small business owner and entrepreneur. However much money you throw at a marketing agency, there are things you must still do to boost your digital brand and take it over the top.

I work in digital marketing in its rawest form, based on performance where real results are demanded, egos bruised and fortunes made. I invite you to read this book and gather insight from my decade of experience at this, the latest frontier of advertising. I hope you will then be able to take the next confident step forward in your entrepreneurial venture or business, through an improved understanding of digital marketing as it relates to unchanging principles in advertising.

SECTION ONE

Yes, Everybody's Doing it

A baby's cry in the night must be addressed. It sounds painful and is designed to annoy. Babies have few options when it comes to getting your attention, and crying happens to be the most effective. Babies refuse to be ignored and their cry is as irritating as it is essential.

Crying is our first advertisement. Everybody does it. Everybody advertises.

Whether the baby needs food, a new diaper, is sick or simply wants to be held, the advertisement is effectively the same. We cry for what we want and need until our final day. The manner in which we advertise changes over time, but the need to do so remains constant.

Take a moment and ask yourself, "How do you cry in your life? How are others crying out, and does it work?"

My children's manner of advertising their needs went from crying to simple sentences, "Want some. Like it. Please." We reinforce the last one, which is our parental way of advertising what we expect from them: politeness, and to join the rest of us in civilized society (after the inevitable, and hopefully brief, adolescent hiccups).

Consider this – crying turns into time at the refrigerator if they are hungry. They may rub their eyes when they are tired, or hold out their arms if they want to be held. Their advertisements change because they realize how ineffective the old ads were. In other words, crying is a great way to get attention, but not always at converting into a sale. In this analogy, at a certain point Mom and Dad (your customers) get sick of the same tactic (crying/cliché marketing ploys) and want you to cut to the chase.

That is to say, you too must adapt your marketing as your company grows.

Chapter One

OUR AD CAMPAIGNS

Let's explore how our quests for attention (our advertising campaigns) work and how others hope we will pay attention to theirs. A sale, in this context, is the acquisition of your desire. You get what you want.

Today we cry into machines. As of writing, the monthly total of people who search for the word "depression" in Google is 368,000. When people make that search, they seek help, and they want to be soothed. Blogs that meet that need tend to do very well in terms of engagement. We once wrote a blog on behalf of a client of ours that ranked number one for the search term "pregnancy quotes," which received over a half million views because it ranked on page one in Google, often in the top three positions. The quotes were positive and soothed readers, not unlike how a mother rocks a baby.

Depression and mortality go hand in hand. Sheldon Solomon, Professor of Psychology at Skidmore College, studies how thoughts of death influence our decisions and judgments. He writes:

> ...one defining characteristic of human beings is self-awareness: we're alive and we know it. Although self-awareness gives rise to unbridled awe and joy, it can also lead to the potentially overwhelming dread engendered by the realization that death is inevitable, that it can occur for reasons that can never be anticipated or controlled."[1]

---

[1]   http://www.scientificamerican.com/article/fear-death-and-politics/

Content that wrestles with mortality, comforting us in the face of the inevitable, is highly shared. Like children, adults want to be comforted, and if a blog does that on whatever the subject, it has a better chance of ranking in Google and receiving more social media shares and engagement.

Whatever you're selling, write blog posts that warm the heart (it's a cliché for a reason) both with their words and the imagery. Create social media posts that comfort your audience and make them feel like everything is going to be okay, and see your shares increase.

Chapter Two

PAY ATTENTION

Currency can be measured in attention. The longer we hold someone's attention, the more money can be made. The best advertisements echo and hold attention long after they've been experienced.

The very best advertisement becomes culture.

The creation of culture is also called "art," and art requires courage. Courage can lead to spectacular success in advertising. Without a willingness to take bold steps to gain attention, you may as well stop trying.

Similarly, if you find yourself giving your attention to aspects in your life that don't return on the attention invested, move on fast. Your time and attention have value. In your professional life, you must measure the profit of putting your energy into what you do. This is simple risk assessment, which every businessperson understands. And it's true in all things, from school, family, work and marketing.

The time you spend looking at something, listening to someone or experiencing something has worth. We create money. Money does not create us. And because we are the creators of currency, we manipulate its value. Our phrase "pay attention" is smart.

To master the ability to hold people's attention over time is to become a leader.

Start by noticing where you pay the most attention. What thoughts do you allow into your life through the media? What are the brands that you most notice? Do you spend a lot of time at Target, Starbucks or Macy's? These brands have their patrons' loyalty (or not) for good reasons. The products a given brand offers might be the best in the market at a given price, but not always. Most likely you are comfortable with a given brand and trust it.

People gravitate to the familiar and known.

From the marketer's perspective, everything is a brand of sorts. This can be a useful way to see our capitalist environment. Your employer is a brand. You have a brand at your job. Call it your "reputation" if you like. Your relationships, taste in music, food preferences, religion and/or political ideology are riddled with brands, brand identities and competing figures. We think of a Donkey when someone mentions "Democrat," an Elephant when someone mentions "Republican" and a cross when someone mention "Christianity." Brands are comprised of messages and symbols, combined to form metaphor, which in turn generates a set of feelings. Much of this happens subconsciously. We don't even notice we've formed these elaborate associations.

Try to imagine "Nike" without the corresponding logo and motto. Hard to do. It's like the old joke: "Don't think of an elephant." Most people see a mental picture of an elephant immediately upon hearing that.

Knowing the world is awash in brands can inspire us to make conscious decisions. Everyone advertises something, and that's okay. What isn't okay is to remain oblivious to that once you know better.

As soon as you understand the motives behind people's actions, you can make informed decisions toward your goals. Likewise, when you advertise, you can respect your audience's intellect, empathize with them and treat them with the integrity people deserve, while serving what they may not even fully know they want until you show them.

Now go ahead. Just do it. And don't think about an elephant.

Chapter Three

AI

When Google announces they've incorporated artificial intelligence into their algorithm, the world should reel. Danny Sullivan from Search Engine Land explains, "RankBrain is Google's name for a machine-learning artificial intelligence system that's used to help process its search results, as was reported by Bloomberg and confirmed to us by Google.

What is machine learning?

Machine learning is where a computer teaches itself how to do something, rather than being taught by humans or following detailed programming.

What is artificial intelligence?

"True artificial intelligence (AI) is where a computer can be as smart as a human being, at least in the sense of acquiring knowledge both from being taught and from building on what it knows and making new connections."[2]

An artificial intelligence that judges our websites should have your attention. Google refers to it as RankBrain and that should be a clue to their intention. A pseudo-mind that determines which

---

[2]   http://searchengineland.com/
faq-all-about-the-new-google-rankbrain-algorithm-234440

websites get traffic and which don't could easily become the major economic force which drives who becomes wealthy and who doesn't.

To think we as individuals might outthink this super-intelligence is laughable. Our intellect doesn't stand a chance. We might be left with this feeling of weakness and confusion, but it doesn't have to be that way. There is only one solid strategy to be employed moving forward, and that is the demonstration of expertise.

Politically, we can argue as to who should own the power of this new mega-mind, but individually we have to recognize it as the judge of our potential fortune. The only evidence this mind can use exists on the Internet as data. The solution then, is to input as much of our analog (non-digital) reality into digital content (data) on the web. This is a terrifying and potentially ugly transition. If privacy isn't dead, it's on life support. And the outlook is bleak. But that's another story, perhaps best left to fiction.

Businesses that are interested in thriving in this new era will have to place an unreasonable amount of information online to not only hold the attention of their potential and current clients, but also appease the demi-godlike brain. It won't be easy.

Luckily, most companies are terrified of giving their employees the ability to market. So, the answer is clear. The entrepreneurs and companies that leverage the expertise of themselves and their employees have a chance to rocket to the top. You can't beat exponential growth. The risk, of course, is that you or an employee says something monumentally stupid and gets you sued. But this can happen anyway.

Some companies will try this employee driven marketing model, and they will get eaten alive because there is no oversight and proper education. But those who develop a curriculum for their employees and review the marketing going out by them will leverage what the Google AI wants: a consistent feed of data.

Right now, the artificial intelligence is clunky and works on inference, making educated assumptions based on the information it has about you. As this process evolves, we will see advanced decision making, beyond that of simple lists of which website ranks the best.

Hold tight, because artificial intelligence is going to be huge politically. It's powerful enough to affect global markets, stocks and economies. Do everything you can now to become an authority online, or you will wish you had once you're buried by others who have.

Chapter Four

RANK ME #1

This covers the basics of SEO (Search Engine Optimization), so that you can audit your work and potentially the work of those you may hire.

Each of the hundreds of businesses I've worked with over the last decade have wanted the same thing -- return on investment. Most believe if they rank well in Google, they will see the desired return. Their success, of course, is completely dependent upon the keywords which they can rank for, the likelihood of getting them there, and what the competition plans to do.

Ranking well in Google is very often the result of a conscious decision to compete in the arena of capitalism, and for anyone to guarantee they'll win that battle is hubris. A certain appreciable quantity of humility goes a long way when determining whether SEO will be a principal driver of revenue for your business. Not only will you have to roll the dice on the SEO team you choose, you are also unable to predict what your competition will do. Staying humble gives you the opportunity to realistically assess your chances.

At Send It Rising, we've taken businesses to the next level through SEO alone. Typically, these clients are already on page two, and we get them into the top three positions for keywords that matter. The results are undeniable. One of our clients is now the proud owner of an estate with a pool, hot tub, built in barbeque, and work garage on a half-acre with statues all over it. When SEO works, it can be a grand slam, and this possibility drives countless business owners and entrepreneurs to give it a serious try.

Tracking revenue from SEO can be a challenge. However, we are becoming more sophisticated with options like CallRail, which allows us to track phone calls and where they've originated. Couple that with website form tracking, and we can paint a fairly accurate picture of ROI.

If you are thinking of starting an SEO campaign, or pushing your SEO further, be sure to install Google Analytics on your website to measure the visitors that are coming to the site, how long they stay, the pages they visit and whether or not they return. You also want to measure how many links you have through Google Webmaster Tools. You may have 10 or 10,000. Then you need to run a ranking report. Install software that allows you to add all the keywords that matter to your business and ensure you can also see the search volume (e.g. the number of people searching for each term). We use Agency Analytics. There is a free tool called CuteRank that I've used as well.

Once you know where your website ranks, you'll be better able to assess your situation and adjust your expectations. If you are on page two for keywords with great search volume, that's excellent! If you are beyond position 100, you've got a long road ahead of you. Don't be discouraged if your website isn't where you thought it would be. Remember that SEO is about building a web asset, and it can be a long process. If you are serious about your business and can plan at least a couple of years into the future, then chipping away at blogs, SEOing your website and creating media will slowly bring you closer to those coveted top spots.

Half of success in SEO is to manage expectations. If you are convinced that you can hire someone that will do SEO for you and that you'll see positive ROI, but you don't know where you currently rank, you have taken that cart and put it before the proverbial horse. Ignorance of SEO, unfortunately, places you in a position to be taken

advantage of. SEO is known for being a gimmicky, unregulated industry filled with charlatans and incompetent salespeople, and for good
reason. Do not fall victim to guarantees or allow yourself to remain
ignorant of what a good SEO program looks like.

At the time I write this, a good SEO program includes writing
the meta titles and descriptions for every page of your website so
they entice potential users to click. Meta titles are the blue links that
appear in Google search results. The meta descriptions are the black
text that appear beneath the blue links in those results.

Landing pages, if not already written, need to be created for every
service your company provides. If you are a mechanic, there need to
be landing pages on oil changes, fixing brakes, check engine lights,
replacement windshield wipers, tires, etc. When someone searches
for those terms, your landing page will have the highest chance of
ranking, and if the page is well made, it will do well in search results
based on the amount of time users spend on the page, whether they
click on other results, come back to the site and hundreds of other
user metrics.

A strong SEO program also includes a consistent flow of new
content, typically centered around a blog. Blog posts are shared
on relevant social media channels including Facebook, Twitter and
Google+. Depending on the business, content is also often shared
on LinkedIn, Pinterest, YouTube and Instagram. In rare cases, Reddit
and StumbleUpon are also good options. There are many more social
media sites to choose from, but these cover the essentials.

"Link building" is a term many SEO consultants throw around
to describe the bulk of the work that we do. Because it is ambigu-
ous, many business owners simply don't probe into what link building is -- this is a mistake. How your SEO consultants link build is
incredibly important, because it will make or break your program. If
you or an SEO company goes about building links using so-called
"black hat" methods (such as creating thousands of articles through

randomizing text), you could be sandboxed from Google and lose years of hard work. On the other hand, should you or your SEO company create some viral images, a tactic we often employ for our clients, you could reap 90% of your meteoric rise from one photo that was shared tens of thousands of times. Honest link building matters.

Google wants to see content people genuinely like. It's that simple.

Chapter Five

HOW LONG UNTIL WE RANK?

This question is understandable. The short answer is that it's difficult to say, and anyone who promises otherwise is selling you snake oil.

MarketingLand.com writes the #1 lie in their article 10 Lies You Should Never Believe From SEO Gurus:

> I Can Get You The #1 Position On Google. Why this lie continues to perpetuate, I'll never understand. Hear this, and hear it well: no one can guarantee rankings on search engines. Except maybe Google, but you're not Google, and neither is that guy you hired to work on your SEO. Google's Webmaster Guidelines state very clearly that you should be wary of SEO firms and web consultants or agencies that guarantee a #1 ranking on Google. Be very skeptical of anyone who promises you top positioning.[3]

To give you a sense of how hard this question is to answer, let's look at a sports analogy. You are considering purchasing a sports team, and you want to know whether or not that team will win the championship or at least place in the top three. The price of the sports team is still being negotiated. The team has never won anything. It's never placed in the top 100 in any tournament. You are going to buy

---

[3]   http://marketingland.com/10-lies-never-believe-seo-gurus-90439

the team and hire one person to come up with a new roster of talent. I happen to be that person. I look at the other teams in the league and do my best to predict whether or not we will win the championship this year, in five years, or ever.

So... how long will it take before we win the championship?

I can tell you whether your competition is relatively strong or weak. However, I cannot now, nor will I ever be able to guarantee search results for competitive keywords, just like no one can predict the outcome of a tournament. If someone is telling you that they can predict the future, be skeptical.

That noted, there are a number of things you can do to size up your competition. Spend time researching your competitors' backlinks. Moz.com has some great tools that allow you to do that.

Do your competitors blog? If so, how often? How many Facebook likes do they have, and are they running ads on Facebook? Do they have a YouTube channel, if so how many videos and views do they have? Are they on Pinterest, Instagram and/or LinkedIn? What does their metadata look like?

If you've never looked at a competitor's metadata, you can go to their site, right click and choose "view source code." The title will be within these tags <title>Title Goes Here</title> and the description will look like this:

```
<meta name="description" content="This is an example
of a meta description. This will often show up in search
results.">
```

Remember that the meta title is the blue link that appears in Google search results and the description is the black text that appears below the blue link.

Knowing your competition is necessary for good business. You may notice that there are competitors holding the top positions who aren't employing any of the strategies that are typically considered best practices. They may have no social media, no blog, and terrible backlinks. In our experience, these competitors will often bounce on and off the front page because they are using unethical black hat techniques.

So how long will it take to rank? More often than not, you are looking at six to eight months to get onto page one for a keyword that matters. If you are on page two already (positions 11-20), you can find yourself on page one within a couple of months. Again, this is pure estimation, but this should give you an idea of what to expect when you engage an SEO consultant.

Chapter Six

50%

We can do approximately half of your Internet marketing, no matter how much you pay us. The other half comes from your customer service and when you ask for reviews, film videos and take pictures. Ranking #1 in Google requires teamwork between the Internet marketing company and the company that retains them. If the marketing department is within the organization, they need to leverage employees outside of the marketing department to get the media needed to share something worthwhile.

As an example, we have a client who has hired someone to write the blogs for their company but doesn't provide her with any pictures. How is she supposed to tell a compelling story without images that relate to the company's work? People don't read blogs: they skim them. So, a blog should contain headers and pictures. And if the person responsible for writing that blog doesn't have access to that media and has to take photos from sites like Shutterstock, we have a problem.

Ranking #1 in Google for a keyword that matters is the cumulative effect of an interesting Internet profile from your blog to Pinterest to Facebook to onsite SEO. These pieces all work together. Google's RankBrain is the smartest entity on planet Earth. It's best we don't underestimate it. So, how can we provide the marketing department or company we've hired the information they need to do a good job? Here's how:

1. Centralize the photos. Make sure your marketing team can easily access every photo that matters. Put the photos in folders that are dated and explain what the pictures are about. Google Drive and Dropbox are good tools for this. Take video. You may not think it's interesting, but for those outside your industry who don't know what it's like behind the scenes, video can be a great way in. Take multiple videos and give your marketing team the option to choose whether the videos have merit. Remember, we're telling a story here.

2. Consistent Content. Your blog should be updated weekly, no excuses. The voice of your company begins with the blog and extends outward into social media. Don't forget social media companies rise and fall. You own your website and need to treat it with respect. Always remember to move all content from the previous site to your new site to maintain the site's value, and insure if your URLs change, redirects are built from old pages to new ones.

3. Focus. Do you know what your marketing team focuses on? What are the keywords that they are targeting, and why are they aiming for those and not others? Months can go by while a marketing team hits the same keywords over and over again. Unbeknownst to them, the company no longer offers what they are pushing. Silly mistakes such as these can be avoided by being clear on the focus. The last thing you want to hear is, "This is the first we've heard of that."

4. Budget. It's pay to play. Many times, clients will say, "Take a look at XYZ competitor. How do we do what they're doing?" The short answer typically is, "Well, they are blogging, spending money on paid media and are actively engaging their social media following." We can't do what they do for $400 a month.

5. Listen. Your marketing team is afraid to tell you everything they know. They are often the first to see that a company isn't doing well, far before the accountants notice a trend. The attention a company gets can easily be seen in Google Analytics, and that attention translates into dollars. If you want to truly grow your company, ask for the brutal truth from your marketing department, and what they know, but won't say unless prompted, may surprise you.

Chapter Seven

WE'RE KIDS

I stand in front of 25 people. I am about to sing a tune from Bubble Guppies, a popular show for toddlers. I've practiced in my car, and I've heard the song countless times before. I want to sing this children's song to this group, because it shows them I care about my family, and I know people do business with those they like.

Outside, outside! Outside, everybody, outside! Line up, everybody, line up, line up, line up, line gup, gup, gup, gup, guppies!

Singing a song for toddlers before a group of professionals could be considered idiotic. But the group's reaction was precisely what I hoped to achieve. They loved it! Why? Because I was being authentic and energetic, and this makes for excellent advertising. Risk-taking and vulnerability are qualities of leadership, and leadership traits are attractive.

It's easy to be vulnerable in your business. It simply takes practice. Let go of the stodgy, uptight, worried emotions and interact with your fans, clients, customers and/or prospects. You may even know most of your fans personally, so why would you distance yourself from them by trying to be something you're not? Share your love for your family, friends and company, and people will resonate with it, because it is relatable.

Recall Dove's revolutionary "Campaign for Real Beauty," which revived the brand. Their PR Company, Edelman, conducted a study of more than 3,000 women in 10 countries to better understand what women value and how they perceive themselves. It came as a shock that only two percent of women considered themselves beautiful, and Dove saw an opportunity for some real, vulnerable, meaningful and ultimately heartwarming advertising. The Dove Campaign for Real Beauty won a handful of awards and contributed to a sales increase to the tune of $1.5 billion.

Now that's beautiful.

Of this, marketing expert Kirsten Nelson writes:

> Dove wasn't touting a revolutionary lotion formula with its campaign. Its product formulas didn't change. And its lotions and creams are much like those of its competitors. The differentiating factor is in the positioning of the product. Dove isn't selling soap. It is selling acceptance and recognition of beauty in women just as they are. Increased sales of soap and related products are the results of this affirmation of normality in women's appearances.[4]

Remember that authenticity, which stems from your life experience, can translate into effective advertising. You can't help but bring what you love into your business, and the more you disconnect the two, the more distance you create between you and your customers.

Be bold. If I can break my own small mold by singing a toddler song in front of a group of professionals, and Dove can break the cultural mold by going against the grain of what the word "beauty" means, you can too.

---

[4]   http://www.newsgeneration.com/2014/04/11/pr-case-study-dove-real-beauty/

Chapter Eight

UNEXPECTED TRAGEDY

A friend of mine is traveling in paradise. She's on a bus during a vacation on a cruise line. The bus gets in an accident, and my friend is badly injured.

She was involved with a networking group I'd joined. When you hear the words "networking group," you may not think about a tight knit, loving community of hardworking professionals working together to collectively achieve their dreams, but that is exactly what my group is. We're awesome.

So, when we heard that our friend was hurt, it really affected us. We stayed in touch with her family and raised money to help with medical bills.

In this particular group, two people typically speak at each meeting. After extensive rehabilitation and healing, our friend was going to come to this meeting, and so we wanted to ensure there would be time for everyone to see her. Because of this, there would only be one speaker -- me.

I knew the day was going to be profoundly meaningful, and that for me to stand in front of my group and pitch all the reasons why they should refer business to me would be inappropriate and possibly even pathetic. I decided regardless of what people might think, I would honor our friend. I chose to tell a story about the last conversation I remembered having with my mother before she passed away.

I practice speeches in my mind. Athletes do the same. The New York Times quotes Nicole Detling, a sports psychologist with the US

Olympic team: "The more an athlete can imagine the entire package, the better it's going to be."

And as Emily Cook, veteran American aerialist puts it, "Visualization, for me, doesn't take in all the senses. You have to smell it. You have to hear it. You have to feel it, everything."

The word "visualization" doesn't conjure up the use of all the senses in practicing a moment in the future. It's more like experiencing the moment before it happens. Call it creative simulation of a desired result.

When crafting this speech, I doubted my courage and the likelihood of me actually pulling it off. I was afraid. I didn't want to cry, but I wanted to express authenticity and passion. There is a thin line between authenticity and over-sharing, between real expression that allows people in and something maudlin that alienates.

I practiced the speech in my car and started sobbing. I was happy about this because I knew any tears shed now would make it more likely I could remain composed for the speech. As I walked in, I saw my friend. She did not look like she used to.   I put my hand on her shoulder and told her that we love her and that we are proud of her. And here's my speech:

"People of the world. First and foremost, on behalf of every sane person on this planet and the universe at large, I would like to say that we love and are proud of you (referring to our friend that was hurt). And in your honor, I'd like to tell the following story. Bear with me. I was in a classroom in North Dakota in the dead of winter. The sun is shining, despite how inexcusably cold it is outside and the rays of light are bouncing into this classroom and onto a piece of art with a silver frame that earns my attention. I get a bit closer and look behind the glass and on parchment it reads, 'I am still learning.' And this moment in and of itself is beautiful, made more so by the fact that moments ago I was attending my mom's funeral. I take the art and it now hangs on my right as I work. Now, the humility it takes a woman who has taught for 20 years to put a piece of art that advertises to her students that 'I too am still learning' is good.

I am going to share with you the last conversation I remember having with her. It goes a little something like this. 'Hey Mom! What's up? I've got this thing going on at ADvise Media Group. I am going to take the job.'"

There were over 30 people in that room and more than a handful cried. The love that I received after giving that speech moved me deeply. People want you to be authentic. You might be able to get away with white lies and telling people what you think they want to hear, but I doubt you'll thrive. The truth simply takes less energy, which you can then use toward your goals. Authenticity is incredibly hard to fake, and moving people to action or to tears requires that you connect with the vulnerable parts of yourself.

Great businesses understand they must be authentic with their audience, and vulnerable. Imagine sacrificing profit for a larger purpose. Seems crazy, but TOMs (the shoes company) did it. They are a for-profit enterprise, and according to TOMs.com they've put 60 million pairs of shoes on children's feet in over 60 countries. You'd better believe their ads tug at your heartstrings and are authentic. They're asking you to spend more than you usually would and trust that they will do the philanthropic work they promise. Their vulnerability is an invitation to share in an authentic experience, and of course to signal to others that you consume consciously. Some might call this cynical, but the results are the same: a powerful brand, happy customers and shoes on the feet of people who need them. Walking solidarity.

Large corporations that don't adapt to this new way of behaving will suffer as they pour money into ad campaigns geared toward the old 30 second T.V. commercial model and compete for the lowest price. Through digital media, companies can earn their customers' attention over hours, online, with heartfelt messaging. We have much more than the 30 second T.V. slots to engage them, and the story needs to be compelling over multiple points of contact, from social media to websites, online video, etc.

I believe empathy is the prime force in the future of advertising. I will be more inclined to buy from you if you demonstrate that you care about making the world a better place. Your online reviews tell the story of whether or not you know what you are doing. You simply can't tell me you are great at your job. The community will do that.

Instead of advertising egotistically, advertise altruistically. Get behind a movement worth your time and energy, and tell that story. We will all be glad you did.

Chapter Nine

ETHAN

As a father of two, my heart breaks when I hear about Ethan, a boy who needed a kidney transplant and follow-up care. Via video, Ethan's mom tells of needing specific medication ASAP. Had it not been for Optum, a health services company, Ethan would be in serious trouble because of insurance companies and industry bureaucracy. The video is a testimonial for Optum and has heart. At the time I write this, it's also Optum's best-performing Facebook post, with four times as many likes as their next-most-popular piece.

This begs the questions, "Have you done something incredible for a client of yours? How willing would they be to write a review or be part of an 'Ethan' video?" Word of mouth has gone digital, and being upstanding, moral and thoughtful has value. If you've done outstanding work for a client, follow up. Whether you realize it or not, they are part of your marketing team and will help you grow your business, if you simply ask. In the new world of links, followers and social shares, your success is also your customers' or clients' success. Share liberally (with permission, of course).

Many of my clients fail to see the power of testimonials displayed on social media. Putting a testimonial on your website doesn't mean much. Those are easily manipulated. Instead, wrack up 100+ Google and Yelp! reviews. The effect on organic rankings, your reputation online and thus sales is measurable. Once my clients realize that a review has real value, they almost always begin to push for them.

In the world of business, the voice of the community can help set you apart from your competitors. The longer, more in-depth the reviews, the better. Who doesn't respond to a good story well told?

And remember that search engines pick up keywords within the reviews, so the SEO benefits of a great set of reviews can be substantial. When happy customers agree to write reviews for you, it's perfectly fine to ask for them to use one or two of the keywords that are vital to your business. Simply ask.

I have a client that has ten times the number of reviews as his nearest competitor, and his phone rings regularly. When asked, "How did you hear about us?" his staff often receives the answer: "Your reviews." The reality is that the reviews are causing the client to rank in Google maps. But what matters to the client is that ringing phone and warm introductions.

The effect of numerous, positive online reviews is twofold: first, you rank higher in search engines because you have reviews and second, you drive more revenue because the customer is more likely to convert. Your happy customers have established your credibility for you.

Ethan's story shows us that testimonials are powerful and can be heartfelt. Do not underestimate the community's voice when advertising your business.

Chapter Ten

IT'S LIKE TV

WCOBM (World Center of Broadcast Media) is the brainchild of Gene Woods, three-time U.S. Open National Speedway Motorcycle Champion. Like a well-crafted, custom machine, Gene has built modular production studios to create turn-key shows. Just like a world-class racer builds a part for their vehicle to be as efficient as possible, Gene and his team have done this for their video production studios, which resemble a branded black mobile home.

The studio I filmed at is in Las Vegas at the Gene Woods Racing Experience. The show that I was on, "The Guy Dawson Show," is about business. We spoke about philanthropy and marketing. These modular production studios are interesting, because in a world driven by social media, the space we desire requires high-end technology.

I tell my clients they should make more videos and send them to us to use online, but they often find themselves unwilling to make public grainy, unprofessional videos. These modular social media video production sets where shows are broadcast live provide a new medium for small business owners to reach audiences. It's a brilliant concept, and time will tell whether or not they become widespread.

The more shows I find myself on, the more I realize that the media professionals are winging it. The typical pre-show routine is quite literally, "Kellen, we're on in 10 seconds." The first time I've spoken to the host is on the air. I've done quite a few of these over the last couple of years and they include:

New Theory Podcast – Real Estate Investment Summit Podcast – That Business Show 2.0 – KDWN 720 AM – PR Connections: Business Edition – Righteous Yammer - The Entrepreneur Way – Dr. Doug Podcast – Money For Lunch Podcast – The Social Celebrity Podcast – Ed Tyll Show – Capital Media HD 99.3 FM, Barbados – Dr. Briar Mitchel Podcast – Profitability Revolution Show - Business Networking International (BNI) – The Growth Mindset Podcast – Planet Hollywood Hotel & Casino – Contractor's Secret Weapon – The How Of Business Podcast – Roseman University of Health Sciences – The Guy Dawson Show (T.V.) – The Lance Tamashiro Show - Las Vegas Real Estate Expo – Lunch & Learn, Leah Martin Law – Something to Chew On Radio Show – American Association of Private Lenders – Small Business Digital Marketing (ITT Tech) – Clark County Association of Health Underwriters – Optimist Leadership Group (Las Vegas Country Club) – IMPACT Learning Conference – Rethink Your Business Las Vegas Podcast – The Philantrepreneur Radio Show

I presume you're good at what you do if you're doing it professionally. So, you must have anecdotes that your audience would be interested in hearing. These anecdotes make ongoing video content simple.

Don't believe that if someone is on a show, they are somehow an infallible expert. It simply isn't the case. Media outlets need guests to fill up time. Don't get stuck on being a perfectionist yourself. If popular radio hosts are winging it on the air, you can improvise with your content as well. You can also enlist the help of your employees or team members to create video content. Just take the time to get everyone on the same page and establish rules of the road. You may want to edit and review anything an employee posts on behalf of the company. That can be a good opportunity not to micromanage but to discuss your company's values and brand, and to ideate together on how you want to present yourselves to the public.

Your video content isn't always going to be perfect, but it will be authentic and your audience is likely tired of the status quo and exhausted clichés. I know I am.

Chapter Eleven

BUSINESS

The way businesses advertise changed profoundly in the decades around the new millennium. The playing field is more level than ever, because the largest companies have to play by the new rules and not all of them are ready.

For example, consider Search Engine Optimization. Google punished JCPenney for creating backlinks, and their rankings tanked. This New York Times article explains the unethical techniques employed by the retailer:

> Despite the cowboy outlaw connotations, black-hat services are not illegal, but trafficking in them risks the wrath of Google. The company draws a pretty thick line between techniques it considers deceptive and 'white hat' approaches, which are offered by hundreds of consulting firms and are legitimate ways to increase a site's visibility. Penney's results were derived from methods on the wrong side of that line...

In fact, many of the links that JCPenney had earned came from sites that had nothing to do with clothing. As the Times article points out, backlinks came from "sites about diseases, cameras, cars, dogs, aluminum sheets, travel, snoring, diamond drills, bathroom tiles, hotel furniture, online games, commodities, fishing, Adobe Flash, glass shower doors, jokes and dentists — and the list goes on.

Even the large players suffer at understanding and implementing Internet marketing. Many times, smaller companies are more equipped to exploit a niche, as they are not bound by the layers of bureaucracy at larger corporations. Smaller companies are also not bound by the interest of the shareholders, who are constantly looking for more value, which adds pressure that can lead a large institution to take unnecessary risks, as in the case above.

Chapter Twelve

RELATIONSHIPS

To say, "You aren't listening to me!" is a way to say, "You aren't paying attention to me." Attention is what we all desire. We often neglect the power of our attention in relationships. Because it is so common, it sometimes doesn't seem like it has much value, but to repeat a point made earlier: currency is attention. To add value to a relationship, always remember you can deposit value by giving attention.

Just as a Fortune 500 company spends millions of dollars to win your attention, realize that your significant others, family members and friends also vie for your "attention dollars".

Oftentimes the more attention someone receives, the more value their attention becomes to others. E.g. Lebron James sits down to hear about how you had a hard day at work. That would be memorable. We, as people, somehow think that because someone is the center of attention, that they have more value. It's odd, but that's how culture works.

People will yell and make dramatic gestures as a form of more engaging advertisement. If someone feels neglected or unheard, their advertising tends to become bolder. It's all about getting the other person's attention.

If your relationship isn't where you'd like it to be, consider your advertising. If you typically get their attention through "Hi, what's up?" you may consider something along the lines of "I've had a very interesting day, but before I share I'd love to hear all about yours."

Now, not only are you advertising that your day was interesting, which is attractive, you also are asking them to describe their day. The time you'll spend in that interaction will probably help the relationship.

We often advertise what we want our significant others to buy for us. "I'd love a treadmill, but they are too expensive" is a clever ad. "I'd love to go to Cancun, but when would we find the time?" is another example. Relationship advertising takes many forms.

Once married, the wedding ring is a commonly accepted advertisement regarding relationship status. People don't always wear their wedding ring, even if they are married, which in itself is an advertisement to the spouse (and others). Problems at home?

Chapter Thirteen

THOUGHTS

As we live, we think. Typically, we don't choose if thoughts enter our minds. Thinking is part of life itself. The basal ganglia, the part of the brain often attributed to habit formation, plays an integral role in where we place our attention. The primary aspect of thinking that we control is whether or not we pay attention to the thoughts at hand. As habits form, we spend less time creating new patterns, which can lead us in good or bad directions. Companies are interested in occupying as much metaphorical space within our basal ganglias, so that our responses become automatic. The more habitual our purchases become, the more likely we are to remain loyal to a brand. We've ceased to choose, and the winner (say, for our daily coffee dollar) can take our loyalty to the bank.

People tend to identify with our thoughts and assume that they are somehow a direct reflection of who we are. In many cases, they more accurately reflect who we were. Learning to advertise some thoughts over others allows us to rewrite our habits, despite years of repeated behavior.

If we find ourselves thinking thoughts that aren't pleasant, we must learn to advertise another thought in its place and/or find a distraction to break the habit loop. As customers, being aware of our habits is vitally important to good decision making. What was the cue that led us to be holding a $4.85 Starbucks for the sixth time this month? How often do we buy from them, and what are the events leading up to us making that purchase?

If we are interested in breaking a habit, we can simply generate and advertise thoughts, ideas and reminders to ourselves which deviate from the typical habit loop. For example, if you want to start exercising in the morning, why not write down your morning workout routine on your bathroom mirror? That's an advertisement to push you toward your goal. Simply having that ad displayed in a prominent location will allow you to break your habit loop. Sure, you may be able to disregard the ad and go about your day, but you'll have given yourself a clear opportunity to close the proverbial deal and begin to build exercise into your routine.

Do this with regularity, and you will find you've created a new habit, which then requires less and less advertising to reinforce. In a way, like a loyal customer with the coffee habit, you'll be accustomed to exercising in the morning. The routine will have made its way to the basal ganglia, allowing you to unthinkingly complete the task at hand, almost as if you were on autopilot.

Chapter Fourteen

FINANCE

5 Acres of Land | Southern California | $99 a month!

"Really? $99 a month? How can that be? What's the catch?"

The seemingly low price holds our attention. Ads that have us thinking about a brand days, weeks and months later convert. A buyer spends their time wishing they had what you have. Before you know it, you've made a sale.

Financing is really a wonderful way to grab attention and to charge them twice what they would have paid if they had the cash on hand.

The low monthly payment is an excellent advertisement, because it can draw in someone's attention by having them believe that they could have what you are selling today. They can afford it right now.

The real estate bubble and subsequent burst of the early part of this century occurred in part due to advertisements by banks. In the years before the crisis, the behavior of lenders changed dramatically. Lenders offered more and more loans to higher-risk borrowers. Before they offered the loans, they advertised them.

We forget this fact at our peril: advertising is not a guarantee. Its purpose is to get your attention!

When the sub-prime lenders got the attention they wanted, they converted it into products that helped cause the financial crisis. The culture advertised its way to a financial disaster the likes of which hadn't been seen since the depression. The origination of this problem was the willingness of the companies to advertise these products, and the consumers who believed them.

As entrepreneurs and business owners, we carry an enormous weight of responsibility for our communities, employees and families. In the rush to success, our advertisements can take on a life of their own and ultimately hurt the people we intend to help. A successful ad campaign is only truly that if the products we are selling are, in fact, a benefit.

Though it is impossible to tell the future, be cognizant of the power you wield as an advertiser, and continue to humbly assess your product to ensure that you are on the right side of history. In other words: place ethics before your advertisement.

Consider financing for your customers, if you don't already, as a means to earn the attention of a much larger pool of people. Financing provides the "have it today" feeling that many consumers are willing to pay more to experience. Services that are typically not financed can be easily converted. Consider for example a website that sells for $3,500. You might be able to earn $4,000 for the same website by offering financing for that site at $333 a month for 12 months. There are, of course, headaches that go along with financing a product, including collecting payment, negotiating terms, and risk of non-payment.

That noted, the more you look at larger purchases, the more often you will find this form of advertising as part of the offer.

Chapter Fifteen

SPORTS

Relationships between team members requires that they minimize overt signals while playing. Let's call those signals advertising. This unwanted "advertising" while playing a team sport is also called "telegraphing." The best team sport athletes are able to hide or mask their intent toward a common goal.

Advertising loudly isn't always the best road to success. Athletes can show us that the most subtle ads can also be the most successful.

In contrast, off the field professional athletes are walking businesses with limited shelf lives. Most have expiration dates, and that's exactly part of the appeal. Some transcend time (e.g. Ali or MJ), but such types are rare. Even the greatest professional athletes will be replaced by up and coming talent year over year. Because of their short careers, the advertising they undertake benefits from a subconscious sense of urgency, and urgency is a critical component to earning attention.

From shoes to milk to music equipment, nearly anything can be sold in an athlete's name. Why? Because they demand so much attention. When millions of people tune into something, you can monetize it. As evolved as we think we are, we are absolutely mesmerized by feats of strength, stamina and dexterity. It's no wonder the world stops for the World Cup, and FIFA seems to always be engaged in some kind of corruption scandal. At that level, the stakes are too high and the money is simply too enticing not to attract bad behavior. And I believe we're secretly drawn to that as well. Sports promises risk and reward with immediacy and tremendous, apparent stakes, both off and on the field.

The most profitable athletes (and their management teams) understand their actions off the field are as important as on, when it comes to advertising their brand. Some athletes' brands become so strong that they begin to see the difference between their public persona and their private self. This common condition of celebrity is caused by our collective attention focused on a select group of people, and the effects can be disastrous for those who don't understand how effective advertising has a dark side.

You have the capacity to create your own celebrity within your industry. Becoming the local expert in your field is how you start. Just as we are drawn to the best of the best in the sports world, we want to know that we're with the best we can get in our communities. A great way to push this is with YouTube.

We've advertised on YouTube for three cents per view. Simple math tells us that $100 will buy you 3,000 views at that rate. Let's suppose that you, like a high-level athlete, want to show the world that either you or your company are the best in the area. Simply set aside $1,000 for a YouTube ad spend, create a few videos showing your expertise, and then only serve those ads to your community. (It's simple to geo target within YouTube ads). By the end of the ad run, you'll have reached 30,000 people in your area. If your videos truly show the best of your company, then you, like a popular athlete, will be drawing in the attention required to own a successful brand.

Chapter Sixteen

CELEBRITY

The reason we strive to earn attention via advertising is to drive revenue. The side effect of powerful advertising, however, is that the people who receive all this desirable attention become celebrities - for better and for worse. Money and celebrity are related. This doesn't mean every celebrity is rich.

It does mean that if they have enough people's attention, they can become rich.

Celebrities often spin out of control because they've advertised well in the past, but their campaign no longer generates the same results. They often then resort to increasingly outrageous stunts to pull in the old levels of attention.

Mercury news reported about Madonna:

> ...she's been doing increasingly bizarre, attention-seeking things during her "Rebel Heart" tour. Like showing up hours late for performances, or acting drunk and rambling incoherently on stage...[5]

Kanye West has become practically synonymous with extreme attention seeking behavior, as ShrinkTank.com reports:

Most are aware of at least one of Kanye's contributions to OMG moments in pop-culture, such as storming out of the American Music

---

[5]   http://www.mercurynews.com/2016/03/18/
dear-madonna-acting-crazy-wont-get-your-son-rocco-back/

Awards in 2004 when he was not voted Artist of the Year; stating that George Bush didn't 'care about black people' post-Hurricane Katrina, and subsequently appearing on the cover of Rolling Stone in a crown of thorns; staging a sales competition with 50 Cent when they both released albums in 2007; his infamous stage invasion during Taylor Swift's acceptance speech at the VMA's when he announced that Beyonce, and not Taylor, should have won the award for best female video; his comparison of himself to Michael Jordan, Steve Jobs, Jesus, etc.; his repetitive, and often nonsensical, declarations of his own genius, vision, and god-like attributes.[6]

Part of advertising well is to understand that once you've earned our attention, you need to tell a story. This is especially true the fifth or eighth time we've come back to your "channel." We want to see how you've grown as a person or company. Reinvent yourself as a better version. The "Nike" of today is not the "Nike" of ten years ago - there's continuity, but it's not the same company. It couldn't survive if it was. Think of Apple, or Google, or Facebook. Facebook twenty years from now will look quite different from Facebook today.

We too need to do this with our personal brands, as do celebrities.

All too often we find celebrities desperately clinging to youth, which may have been why we paid attention in the first place, but not why we will pay attention now.

I started my career as an ESL (English as a Second Language) and Spanish teacher. I'd return home after work and write on one of two websites: Associated Content and Bright Hub. Both sites allowed authors to earn passive income based on the number of site visits they generated from their articles. This was my introduction to blogging. SEO, as far as I knew back then, consisted only of the "SEO Title" and "SEO Description."

I began blogging on top of a teaching career 10 years ago.

[6] http://www.shrinktank.com/psychologists-perspective-kanye-west/

I moved to Las Vegas and took a job for $9 an hour with a small company: ADvise Media Group. I got the job because I'd earned tens of thousands of views from my articles on Bright Hub and Associated content. I took a job teaching at night and would take naps in between my two jobs, which I needed to make ends meet.

I rose through the ranks at ADvise Media Group, eventually becoming a partner, and then founding my own company: Send It Rising Internet Marketing. If I'd clung to what worked 10 years ago I would not be where I am now. When I was standing in front of a crowd at Planet Hollywood Hotel and Casino, being paid to speak to them, I recall thinking "This has been years in the making."

We're pursuing celebrity by taking it a step further and have purchased space on digital billboards throughout Las Vegas to create buzz around the Send It Rising brand and KellenKautzman.com. Just recently I received an email for a potential speaking engagement that pays $3,000 for 90 minutes, in part because the of buzz created from the billboards.

Wherever you find yourself now, remember that you can earn attention through solid work, entrepreneurship and being courageous. Don't forget that not taking risks is risky! You can become a celebrity in your space, a thought leader and a visionary.

Just keep one eye on your integrity and don't sell it.

Chapter Seventeen

FANTASY

We live in our heads. As such, we tend to gravitate toward thoughts that speak to our dreams and fantasies. Feeding fantasies is a multi-billion dollar industry, regarding wish fulfillment in general and sex especially. If anyone convinces us, even for a moment, we can achieve our dreams, we become hooked. Once we've bought the deeper message, we're addicted.

Tell us what we want to hear, and we'll follow, generally speaking.

Religion certainly doesn't have a monopoly on fervent believers. The world of Self Help has followers as fanatic as any religion (just without the tax break). We love the idea of fantasy and dreams come true. From cartoon princesses to Jedi, fantasy captivates us. And it's no wonder that the merchandizing from these fantasies is where the real money is made. It's one thing to capture someone's attention. It's another thing to monetize on it. That is: to make it real.

Monetizing fantasies is as simple as realizing what people commonly fantasize about. Sex is the obvious first answer, as of course it comes with accompanied fantasies. Outside of sex, people fantasize about retiring early and being rich, eating luxurious food and having time to pursue their hobbies. Pinterest.com, with 150 million active users, is a website for visual wish fulfillment. From the most delicious pastries in the world, to beautiful men and women, high fashion and luxury homes, Pinterest gives its users the images they perhaps didn't even know they wanted.

Tai Lopez starts his YouTube videos for his courses by taking viewers through a tour of his mansion or washing his fleet of luxury cars. I find the approach garish, but he's earned over 800,000 subscribers and recently had pop star Rihanna on a video.

Books like The Secret and Think and Grow Rich, which focus in on the concept that what we think we create, and the so-called "law of attraction" hit our fantasy nerve. Customers delve into a fantasy world and leave feeling energized about possibilities. Advertising fantasy is a multi-billion-dollar business that plays on our desires. TV shows like Friends play into a "New York City" fantasy, the result of which is that we end up watching our television "friends" instead of hanging out with our real (or even Facebook) ones.

Fantasy extends beyond money and sex and into science fiction, another massive genre that plays to fantasy. Anything that draws us from this world and into another is a type of advertising, as it pulls in and moves our attention from ourselves to something external and abstracted. Movies are commercials for themselves, for their own "brand." They are feature length commercials we pay to see. What a concept! The commercial is for all the shirts, toys and games that are going to follow the movie. Many of those items, especially the shirts and Halloween costumes, are yet more advertising. And what a coup if you can get consumers to purchase advertisements for your product, and proudly wear them.

For example, I own a Jurassic Park shirt which I purchased when Jurassic World was released. Within my subconscious is a childhood connection to that movie. I, as a child, wanted to be a paleontologist after seeing that film. Years later, the executives in charge of delivering Jurassic World managed to get Jurassic Park merchandise into stores. Branding runs deep, and my (let's be honest: somewhat unrealistic) fantasy of being a paleontologist as an elementary school kid was strong enough for me to buy a shirt decades later.

Some of your favorite things are a type of advertising. I type this on an Apple laptop, which of course advertises and sells itself to anyone who sees the logo, with its sleek form factor and the corresponding status implied in the brand. The same device in a different box presents a different image to the world.

Remember that not only can we use fantasies to earn attention and offer our target audience a product or service, but we are also constantly bombarded by advertising that attempts to do that very same thing to us. We are awash in symbolism. Are the fantasies that you hold your own, or are they the cumulative effect that ads have had on you over the course of your lifetime? It's worth a pause to reflect and check in on this, if only to consider your own fantasies and reflect on where you may have forgotten something that motivates you powerfully, without your even noticing.

Chapter Eighteen

OPTIMISM

The Secret, the Law of Attraction, and books like Napolean Hill's Think and Grow Rich have done a number on our collective consciousness, advertising that we can achieve our dreams. We just need to refocus our minds and imagine ourselves already in possession of those things.

I'll be the first to admit that I've been using the law of attraction in my life for years, advertising positive thoughts in my mind to attain the goals that most interest me.

The only problem is that there is a cost to that advertisement. What is the cost behind the law of attraction? Because none of us exist in a bubble, our actions have a direct impact on those around us. They too dream. Many times, our dreams and their dreams come to a cross-roads.

Take the example of everyone who dreams they will someday become the President of the United States of America. Very few will, but many will envision it. Conflict ensues when competing visions collide. The quantity and quality of our dreams come into contact with the dreams of others, and space is made for the victor. And so, many of us give up on our dreams over time.

Having positive thoughts consistently is a lot like managing a complicated advertising campaign. You constantly have to assess the return on investment, which varies over time. If you spend nearly every waking moment envisioning your goal and you see no return, you may become discouraged and give up. Alternatively, there are those who, despite no returns, continue to dream. We tend to only hear about those who succeed. What about those who continue advertising their dreams with no return? They are often lumped into the category of "in denial" or "hopeless." Nobody wants to be that.

Being able to judge your return by implementing the law of attraction is important and reasonable. I wholeheartedly believe in goal making, envisioning a better future and working to attain it. I also believe in making rational decisions and cutting yourself some slack if a plan does not turn out how you'd planned it.

Chapter Nineteen

MUSIC

If you've ever seen a great band perform, you know that it's hard to look away. Great bands really master their advertising (their performance) for however long they'll be onstage. They know the songs you've come to hear, and they sense and understand your expectations. The concert itself is an advertisement, and you know there are a few items for sale at their merch shop, conveniently located where you can't possibly miss it on the way out. And of course, they have a website that sells their merchandise too.

A "sell out" is a term we throw around a lot to describe a band that advertises too often or makes too much money. It's a term that inevitably gets deployed once a band achieves a certain level of success. We see art and advertising as polar opposites, when the reality is that all art is an advertisement. Although all advertising is not art.

As Jason Newsted, bassist for Metallica famously said: "Yes, we sell out...every seat in the house, every time we play, anywhere we play."

Within this statement lies the insinuation that "selling out" is bad and that it somehow needs to be justified. This is sentimental nonsense.

If art wasn't an advertisement, no one would ever see or hear it. The second someone else encounters art, it becomes an advertisement for itself. Because art needs to be talked about to be considered art at all. If a painting sits in a closet, what is it? Junk.

Thinking of bands as advertisers can help us understand their struggle. They must find a way to get and hold people's attention, oftentimes for very little pay. Their career depends on how well they advertise on and off stage.

The band's lead singer is oftentimes the head advertiser, and it's very often up to them to hold the crowd's attention. Many of these head advertisers will get the crowd to clap along with them when the time is right. They will speak to a crowd to hold their interest and have the audience sing along. These are all efforts to keep the elaborate advertisement for their music engaging. It's spectacle.

No wonder pop and rock musicians oftentimes wear clothes that off stage are ridiculous. Dramatic clothes hold our attention. You can probably name no fewer than three bands off the top of your head whose clothes stand out in your mind. Even plain clothes are a statement, when given the massive amount of attention a popular band receives onstage. Our minds fill in the gaps and ascribe meaning even when there is none intended.

Courage is a prerequisite to good advertising, and musicians are clearly courageous. Imagine standing in front of 10,000 people with everyone chanting your name. That will get your heart beating. What if you miss your cue or forget the lyrics or lose your lunch right before a big solo?

Great advertising shifts the consciousness of a large group for the moments in which you captivate them, but also for an immeasurable period of time after the ad stops. We go to live music hoping to see a great show but to also acquire memories we'll take home. "I saw Pearl Jam on their first tour," can spark an evening of conversation at a bar with a stranger. This has value.

Some of the best music will remain in the cultural consciousness for generations to come. Those advertisements are played and replayed because even today they hold our attention and are worth sharing. Name a bigger global brand than the Beatles or the Stones.

Just as a musician can captivate an audience, you too can earn and hold the attention of potential current customers and clients. Imagine creating a YouTube video, with music, that in less than two minutes teaches the viewer something they didn't know about your industry, and which also entertains and leaves them feeling empowered.

Can you see how, despite how boring your business may seem to you, that you can be a star in your own right? Andy Warhol was correct. We're all going to get our fifteen minutes. Why not make yours work for your business?

Chapter Twenty

GIVE THEM THE POWER

As a teacher, I often thought about ways in which I could empower my students. I was able to learn Spanish in part because I watch English movies with Spanish subtitles. This one switch in my behavior has drastically improved my Spanish over the years.

In a similar vein, how might we empower ourselves to advertise more effectively? How do we empower our employees?

I was raised by two teachers, and the complaints they brought home were endless. Complaining about students is practically a part time job for many teachers. When I became a teacher, I realized that much of the anxiety comes from not being able to help a student that has no interest in my subject. As a Spanish teacher, much of my time was spent advertising the benefits of Spanish. It doesn't matter to the students that the University of Minnesota gave me a piece of paper that says, "Master's Degree in Education" on it.

The classroom is a challenge because, unlike the business world, the students are often without choice. I moved into business because I enjoy the idea of working with people who are interested in being in the room-- that is, people who want to advance and be successful.

My first career was in education, and in many ways, I am still an educator. We teach clients how to create media their audiences will take an interest in. The classic example is a Facebook post: one that is a standard "10 Things You Didn't Know About [Insert Relevant Topic Here]." We've created thousands of these, because they work. They get a moderate amount of traction and help raise rankings in

Google, which makes the phone ring. It's a little boring, yes, but it gets the job done.

What we really love to see is the second kind of Facebook post, one that goes behind the scenes of a business to show customers the faces behind the company. The ideal post includes the employees happily helping others in the community through social engagement on behalf of the company. Feeding the homeless is a wonderful example of that.

Just as I engaged my students, my team and I engage audiences, providing them with information. Getting your customers to help promote your product is truly the "secret sauce," because it can grow your advertising departments' size exponentially. This only occurs if you have a good product! You can advertise the benefits of SPAM all day, every day, but you are going to hit a plateau based on the fact that you're selling a product that is only probably meat. In other words, all markets have their limits.

Companies that restrict their employees' social media profiles baffle me. I understand that brand integrity matters, but when you hire someone, you are already potentially compromising the brand's integrity by taking a risk. Each employee is an extension of a company's brand. The key is to have your employees fall in love with the company because the company is doing incredible things. This is one of the many reasons why we launched a comprehensive Cause Marketing initiative. Cause Marketing focuses on bringing nonprofits and businesses together to help promote one another. Employee retention occurs, in part, because the employees feel part of something larger and philanthropic.

Let's imagine a new wave of companies that understand the interconnectivity of the web, SEO in particular. They provide each of their employees the opportunity to send in posts (to be approved) for the company's social media channel and ask them to take pictures and make YouTube videos. Imagine a company that consistently provides their employees with volunteer opportunities, or even creates a philanthropic budget that allows for their employees to spend time giving back. Thousands of photos and videos are waiting to be taken and the impact on social and SEO would be staggering, exponential in fact.

Now, there are restrictions to what can be done, but they aren't so strict that it's no longer fun to do. A brand is simply an idea that people share and when the employees of a business have no say in the branding of the company they work for, there is a disconnect. Companies that leverage the willpower of their employees online will take the lead.

This is how we return to education. A curriculum that fully shows employees how they can promote the business which they are a part of will encourage them to become involved in marketing socially. I recommend a barrier between the employees' posting directly to the social media platforms, i.e. an editor, but that's it. Give them direct access to the people in charge of the social media. They'll feel more empowered and can also use successful posts as a resume builder. This is especially important for salespeople.

An example from the real estate world. If I own a Real Estate Brokerage with 100 real estate agents and don't allow them to own their own websites, I am missing out on web equity. All of the websites that are built within a company can work together, just like a master plan community, to drive value and ultimately increased equity. If I give my people the ability to have their own sites and provide them with a curriculum through which they can create and manage their own successful blog, image and video content, now I own assets that my employees are building for me. We all benefit.

It's rare to see companies willing to take the risk to give their employees a say in the business. All too often the companies leave the voice of the company to the marketing department, which is the typical way to addressing communication. Here is the problem: the marketing department is only one group of people. In the real estate brokerage example, let's say that all 100 real estate agents are given access to a series of training courses online that walk them through how to promote their business online. Not all of them will take advantage of this opportunity. Those who do are more likely to excel, and the brokerage can highlight their achievements, getting the other real estate agents interested in the potential return on their time investment.

It's all about education and empowerment. Don't be afraid to encourage your employees to be social, within bounds, and see your SEO ranking and social engagement improve.

Chapter Twenty-One

FAMILY

Who is getting the most attention? You would think that the kids would be the ones most strongly fighting for attention, but do not forget that parents are prone to acting childish too. The advertising campaigns that go on under the roofs of our homes require a tremendous amount of resources. When properly filmed, they make for great reality TV.

The baby cries, advertising the need for food, to be held, etc. Meanwhile, the toddler also feels the need to melt down, advertising how unfair it is that the baby's advertising is more effective. The parents meanwhile advertise how exhausted they are to one another with loud sighs and postures that'd play better on the Walking Dead than in the living room.

These elaborate ad campaigns are designed to sell the other family members on the importance of each other. Because families spend so much time together, the ad campaigns often become so irritating that they cause disturbances. For the same reasons that you wouldn't want to watch the same commercial 135 times, you can see why families struggle with giving one another the attention they desire.

A failed ad campaign on the behalf of a child trying to earn their parents' attention can result in a disorder that Billi Gordon Ph.D. elaborates on in his Psychology Today article:

From our beginnings as babies, we explore complex transactions with our families as we try different ads to see what works best. We learn the hard way that things change. As we grow older, crying alone no longer results in a sale. People eventually start ignoring us.[7]

How does this translate to your business? Think about advertisement freshness and how important that is. If you find yourself repeating the same advertisements, expecting the same results, you may be behaving like a toddler that is crying like a newborn. What worked last year may not work again today. Running the same commercial over and over again becomes annoying quickly. Freshen up your ad.

Now this doesn't mean it will work better guaranteed. It does mean that you'll at least stop running the old ad that everyone is sick of. Keep running the same ad and people will likely tune you out.

Here is a good example of that transition within a family setting. Suppose that you always say, "I work really hard and I just need time to relax."

Let's assume that this ad, despite repeated attempts, is not returning results. Now suppose that you update your ad's language to the following:

"I've accomplished _____ today, including _____, _____, and _____ and I would love a moment to unwind. I am happy to return the favor in fifteen minutes."

The same essential message is being delivered, but the second is interesting, more thought out, more performative and empathetic and so more likely to result in a sale. The first is boring, repetitive and predictable. Remember, advertising is about entertaining your audience and holding their attention.

Karl Greenberg, author on the Media Post, references a survey:

---

[7] https://www.psychologytoday.com/blog/obesely-speaking/201411/excessive-attention-seeking-and-drama-addiction

[of] 1,000 consumers and marketers, the study showed that just about all consumers, rather than being likely to turn a cold shoulder, actually want to engage with brands. Brands that don't vary the message turn people off. Half of consumers in the study said if they see or hear the same ad over and over again, it makes them shut out the brand. [8]

Let's take a moment and analyze how kids advertise. Toddlers are advertising geniuses straight out of Mad Men. A toddler will negotiate with you based on what you pay attention to. If you don't want a toddler climbing on the couch, well guess what? That's where they'll spend most their time. Why? Because they are advertising successfully. They instantly grab your attention by climbing on the sofa, and they can then get you to give them something in exchange for not doing that anymore, and even if that doesn't work, at the very least they got your attention.

Toddlers are such great advertisers that their parents will research how to better negotiate with them. James Lehman, in his article Living with Little Lawyers: Don't Over-negotiate with Your Child describes a typical bedtime conversation:

"the over-negotiating parent will say, 'It's time to go to bed. It's 8 o'clock.'

And the child says, 'Oh Mom please, this show's really important, can I just stay up until 8:30 tonight, I just want to watch the end,'

The mom says, 'No, you have to go to bed now.'

The child continues to argue: 'Oh please, please, you never let me do anything. Just ten more minutes.'

The mother relents: 'OK, if you promise not to give me a hard time.'

And the child says, 'Thanks, Mom. You're the best.'

---

[8]   http://www.mediapost.com/publications/article/159757/
woo-buyers-with-paid-owned-earned-media.html

The parent goes back and forth with the child, when really, there's nothing to negotiate here. Let me be clear: the more you give in to negotiating with your child, the more you're training your child not to accept your limits."[9]

From my perspective, the child in this example is simply a better businessperson!

This kind of behavior, advertising to others through doing the "wrong thing" persists through life. Sometimes, later in life when someone is struggling they will advertise in a violent, often self-destructive way. Call this a cry for help. These very serious advertisements are designed specifically to draw as much attention as possible.

Ignoring unwanted ads is a necessary skill. Remember, ads require energy. As a kid, it's protesting, as an adult in a business setting it can mean literally managing a million dollars in pay per click spend, or a simple print ad in the local paper. Either way, an ad that doesn't earn someone's attention is pointless. If you don't like someone's ad, consider simply ignoring it. If your ads aren't converting, switch them up.

Get creative. Or hire someone to get creative for you. Even better: hire someone to get creative with you. You'd be surprised what a session or two with an advertising copywriter or digital advertising expert can generate. It doesn't need to cost you Park Avenue money to get good, creative results. Think now about all the creative people you know who are good writers, actors or artists of another stripe. Book their time and brainstorm. Think about your audience and what would grab their attention. And try it.

As an entrepreneur or business owner, get ready to switch up your advertising often! It is a continuous puzzle to be solved. If you

---

[9]   https://www.empoweringparents.com/article/living-with-little
       -lawyers-dont-over-negotiate-with-your-child/#

keep cranking out the status quo, people may be shouting at your ads out of sheer annoyance. Be open to attempt new things, and be willing to receive criticism from those to whom you advertise. The sound of crickets or a ringing phone will tell you how you've done. Your audience may love or be indifferent to your ads. What works in the infancy of your business will probably not work as it matures. Your company will grow, just like your family, hopefully into messages that resonate with your maturity level.

SECTION TWO

ADVERTERE

Advertere is a latin work that means "to turn toward." It is the root of the word "advertising." Anything that causes you to turn toward it is an advertisement. From the laptop screen to an unexpected sound, the vibration of your cell phone to friend saying your name -- all ads.

Advertising isn't inherently good or bad, effective or ineffective. Open your mind to what advertising is, and you will find it everywhere. You will realize that it is not the object you are selling that will determine your success, but rather your ability as an advertiser to earn attention with available media. Internet marketing, SEO, PPC, web development, blogs, influencer marketing, inbound marketing and a slew of other buzzwords are synonymous with the word "advertisement." They are variations on a theme.

We swim in advertising. As an example, you are a walking advertisement for the way you make a living. I often tell Mary Kay Consultants that they simply need to be incredibly social with their target market. If someone knows you are a Mary Kay Consultant, you don't need to hard sell them every time you see them. They know what you do. Be a part of their lives, because they surely have someone in their life who uses beauty products. How likely they are to refer you is the real question. As a realtor, relationship building is essential, yet many real estate agents focus on developing relationships only with those looking for homes! At any given moment, within everyone's network, is a person in the market to buy property. Whether a person is willing to put their reputation on the line to refer you is the best test of your advertising ability.

I find myself in networking groups filled with people who are just starting out. They are wide eyed about the possibilities in their industry, and so typically go right into selling their product. For those of us who have been successful at advertising and business building, we know six months is a completely reasonable life cycle for the sale of a large product. Measuring all the touches that occur prior to a sale is complicated, and despite having incredible tools like Google

Analytics and Webmaster Tools, Facebook analytics and call tracking through sites like CallRail.com, we still are largely clueless as to the number of times a client has heard about us before they make that first purchase.

For this reason, I recommend to those of you who are starting out: please understand your first conversation with a potential client is your opportunity to advertise how good of a listener you are. Typically to solve someone's problems, you need to be aware of their situation. Nothing shuts down a sale like remaining ignorant of the client's situation. You can beg for customer's attention all day, but if you don't listen to them, they will ignore what you have to say. It's like a first date. You don't want to do all the talking!

Most potential customers are uncomfortable being sold. As business public speaker Jeffery Gitomer puts it: "People don't like to be sold, but they like to buy."

Once you've established you work for, or own, XYZ company, rapport becomes more important than the product or service. Your advertisement should be that you are a good listener and that you are interested in the details of their problem so that you can better understand how you may be able to fix it. Be a consultant, not a salesperson.

Try not to think of advertisement as something to promote things you buy, or some fancy new platform on the web. Advertising is part of who you are, and you've been doing it your entire life. Think creatively about how you can earn people's attention.

For example, Facebook allows us to retarget potential clients who have visited our website. So, we create an ad that appears in their Facebook feed that isn't designed to have them purchase anything in that moment. It's informative, reminding them that we are a comprehensive Search Engine Optimization, Social Media, Pay Per Click and Web Development solution. We actually prefer that they don't click on the ad, because we're charged when they click.

We want to rack up the number of times our logo is seen alongside our services, because we know that it's going to take multiple impressions to convert to a sale. We're not selling a $10 product. An ongoing, monthly service like ours is an investment for businesses, and they are right to want to digest our ads over time and deeply vet our services before they jump.

Envision courageous actions you can take to inspire others, and you'll become a master advertiser, a leader, and a successful entrepreneur. Our company has created videos for YouTube every week for months. It began with a desire to be creative. As the months pass, we've had ups and downs. Friday afternoons are the time we carve out to create the videos, and each Friday is wildly different. Some are relaxed, while others verge on panic. But because complex sales require multiple touches, it's vitally important to have stability in your advertising. Had we created videos for a couple of months and then dropped off, we never would have seen the growth we've experienced. And don't forget how unreasonably cheap YouTube views are. We've gotten views for as low as two cents. If you can afford $5 on coffee, you can advertise on YouTube.

But advertising goes far beyond commercials on YouTube, radio spots, billboards, Pay Per Click, web development, and SEO. Because an exchange of money is simply an agreement between people, you have to become trustworthy, and that comes with consistency. How much energy are you willing to put into your business every week so that it grows? Exponential growth is great, and we experienced that... for a time. But all growth eventually finds a plateau, and the way in which you advertise has to remain strong throughout the peaks, valleys and plateaus of your business.

We may not like it, but advertising is a staple of our existence. As an entrepreneur or business owner, set a growth goal and find a pace that you can maintain for the next two years. If you decide that you are going to have a blog, excellent! Let's see posts for the next

24 months -- no exceptions. If YouTube sounds like a good idea to you, wonderful! What can you do today that will help you plan for the next two years of video creation? How many ideas can you come up with to set you up for success over the next two revolutions around the sun? Set goals. Make a production calendar, and stick to it. You'll thank yourself later.

Chapter Twenty-Two

MAKE YOUTUBE VIDEOS

SEO is a battle. Every advantage counts. I tell my clients that I need them to start creating YouTube videos. As reported in ITechPost. com:

> YouTube has recently disclosed its most updated statistics and the Internet giant claims that its website gets one billion hours worth of views per day. In a blog post, YouTube's VP of Engineering, CristosGoodrow, has expressed his pride and gratitude for the website's success. He says that this achievement indicates the enjoyment people get from the site.[10]

A billion hours per day cannot be ignored, and yet many businesses still live in a world where a YouTube video is considered to be more like a TV commercial than an online video. Quantity matters online. In the television age, you had 30 seconds, and that cost you handsomely. Now you've got as much time as you'd like to push forward regular content. For many small and mid-sized businesses however, the fear of creating videos or being the face of the company is paralyzing.

As a young person, I thought that being self-conscious would evaporate after high school, perhaps college at the latest. Not so. The reality is that most people feel self-conscious throughout their entire

---

[10]   http://www.itechpost.com/articles/88956/20170228/youtube-gets-one-billion-hours-worth-views-per-day.htm

lives, and YouTube heightens feelings of insecurity. Our faces online, talking about whatever, is a nightmare scenario for many people. As Nick Morgan of Forbes.com points out:

> About 10 percent of the population loves public speaking. That group experiences no fear and get a huge buzz being in front of a large crowd.
>
> Another 10 percent are genuinely terrified. Those are the people who are physically debilitated by even the thought of public speaking. True glossophobics will go to great lengths to avoid speaking in a group situation, and will experience nausea, panic attacks and extreme anxiety.
>
> The rest of us — roughly the 80 percent in the middle — get butterflies, get anxious, don't sleep much the night before — but we know that we're going to live through it. It's just not much fun.
>
> That fear we experience — whatever the precise physical symptoms — is adrenaline-based. That means that it's unpleasant but not debilitating. Here's the good news: with a little work, we can turn those butterflies to our advantage.[11]

Nick is right. To overcome fear of public speaking is paramount for Internet entrepreneurs and business owners. YouTube is simply too large and powerful to be ignored, and there are significant SEO benefits to having YouTube videos and links in the description area of the video and annotation links. (Annotations are the notes that appear within the video that you can click on. Annotations often include a link to another video, the website, or the option to subscribe to the channel.)

---

[11]   https://www.forbes.com/sites/nickmorgan/2011/03/30/why-we-fear-public-speaking-and-how-to-overcome-it/#6d5ba678460b

Business owners are experts in their industry, and yet speaking in front of a camera is horrifying for many of them. You can turn this to your advantage! Simply answering basic questions on YouTube and embedding those videos within your site's blog gives you an advantage.

It is still very much the wild west online, and the opportunities are massive. I really thought YouTube would have become much more competitive more quickly, but small businesses are so busy with everything else that marketing, and especially YouTube marketing, takes a back seat if it gets a seat at all.

Many business owners I've chatted with have no idea what the average cost per view is for YouTube ads. For us, it's hovered around three cents. And we are only charged if the viewer watches for over 30 seconds or clicks on one of our links. We've received 70,000 impressions and 4,000 views for $140. I've been recognized randomly here in Las Vegas based on the YouTube videos I've been advertising!

Bottom line: start making YouTube videos! They are assets that will stand the test of time. They also build links back to your website through annotations. If fear is stopping you from moving forward, download a video program (I use iMovie) and record a tutorial on something you do every day. You will have to get used to your voice and seeing your face on camera. It is well worth it. If you are serious about Internet marketing, low cost video production is key! Fight the fear and make more videos.

Chapter Twenty-Three

GROUPTHINK & REVIEWS

If my business has 143 positive Google reviews and the nearest competitor has 3, who would you choose?

We are wired to assume the crowd is making the right choice. As reported in Forbes:

> ... when people didn't have a strong opinion about the choices presented to them, they simply mimicked the people around them. Rather than asking questions, or spending time learning about products, people deferred to the "social default."[12]

It's really quite easy to get someone interested in your business. Just prove to them that many others are also interested. Reviews are an easy way to do this, and we live in a golden age of Google reviews. They are exceptionally simple to earn. Right now, it's as easy as asking for someone with a Google account (and who doesn't have one?) to write you a review and eureka, you've got one. I often ask clients if they would be willing to write me a review. I will borrow their phone with permission, navigate to the page where we can write the Google review and hand the phone back. No one has said no to me yet.

---

[12] http://www.forbes.com/sites/amymorin/2014/07/25/study-shows-the-power-of-social-influence-5-ways-to-avoid-the-herd-mentality/#65adbfab2495

Yelp, on the other hand, might be the most ridiculously strict platform on the web in terms of reviews. It's a nightmare. Yelp is like a bouncer in front of an exclusive club. Only pretty girls and famous guys get in. Yelp will only allow a review if it passes their strict metrics, which include how long the reviewer has had a Yelp account, the number of reviews they've written and the quality of the review, etc.

Yelp even goes so far as to tell businesses, "Don't ask for reviews." A page on their website clearly states so.

Yelp's recommendation software is designed to highlight reviews from people inspired to share their experiences with the community. Most businesses only target happy customers when asking for reviews, which leads to biased ratings. So, the recommendation software actively tries to identify and not recommend reviews prompted or encouraged by the business.

Great! The idea is that we shouldn't advertise at all and just pray? I think not. If I know someone who has a Yelp account and they are willing to write a review for our business, or one we represent, we will definitely ask for their review.

That said there are a number of elements that go into a good review. Checking in, photos and a story is what Yelp is looking for. "Amazing food! They are best restaurant in Las Vegas!" That isn't going to cut it. On the other hand, this will work:

> "We've been visiting XYZ restaurant for a couple of years now and we always ask for the same waiter, Sean. He's memorized our order by this point and even knows that we want one Korean street taco, even though they usually come in threes. The all you can eat option is our favorite and the salmon nigiri is out of this world. If you are planning on eating here on Friday, make sure to make a reservation ahead of time. They book up fast. In all likelihood, we'll be eating here a few years from now."

Include a picture of Sean the waiter, check in and you are on your way to a solid review that doesn't get stuck in the review filter.

I have to tip my hat to Yelp. Many of my clients ask, "Should I spend $500 a month on a one year contract with Yelp?" and they seriously think about it. What other product, car, home, service can simply add you to a website and demand $500 a month for a year and force you to seriously consider it? Incredible. Just today, I was chatting with an attorney who said this: "It's basically extortion. When I pay Yelp, my reviews magically start appearing." He was referencing a typical grievance that many business owners have with Yelp. The reviews don't stick. Whether or not Yelp actually changes their algorithm based on whether you pay is up for debate.

Many times, a Yelp profile will outrank the competing website for major keywords. This drives clients crazy. "How can Yelp outrank my site?" they wonder. It may have something to do with ludicrous number of links Yelp has pointing back to it, their user engagement, and just how robust these profiles can become. I've seen Yelp profiles with over 200 photos and 300+ reviews. That is a lot of content. Couple that with the authority of the site and you have a winning formula.

The downside for Yelp is that at any moment, Google can update the algorithm, perhaps because they feel threatened. Poof, if you're relying on Yelp, then you're out of the top search results. When I work for clients, I put my money on the website they own. I've always preferred building my own assets, my websites that I control over time instead of giving the power to the big players. Clearly, we have to work within the parameters set by Facebook, Twitter, Google +, Yelp, Pinterest, LinkedIn and the countless other social media sites that crop up, but I consider those side bets to the main action: the primary digital asset you own and control, which is your website. The site(s) you own is ultimately your only digital asset. Once we've earned the attention of your audience, we want them to visit your site, not someone else's.

The first reviews will be the hardest. Actively pursue reviews, knowing that once you've established a rhythm, momentum will pick up. Having more reviews than your competitors will instill within potential customers and clients the sense that more people trust you, that you are the better choice, and that they are smarter if they choose you. That mentality is deeply ingrained in our psyches. What the majority of people choose attracts our attention. Having more reviews than your competitors is wonderful advertising.

There are companies that will integrate into your website the option for potential and current customers to leave a review. BirdEye is an example.

Beyond this, earning reviews remains a personal endeavor for most small businesses. The business owner or salesperson simply exchanges their relationship capital for a review. According to Google, here are the ways they'd prefer you to get your reviews:

> Remind your customers to leave reviews. Let them know that it's quick and easy to leave business reviews on mobile devices or desktop computers. Reply to reviews to build your customer'strust. Your customers will notice that your business values their input, and possibly leave more reviews in the future. You can also create and share a link that customers can click to leave a review. Learn how to read and reply to reviews. Verify your business so your information is eligible to appear on Maps, Search, and other Google services. Only verified businesses can respond to reviews.[13]

Replying to reviews is an often underutilized strategy for many business owners and entrepreneurs. Don't just respond to bad reviews. Responding to good reviews is equally as important. Remember that

---

[13]   https://support.google.com/business/answer/3474122?hl=en

every word written that relates to your business is being measured by Google's artificial intelligence algorithm RankBrain.

When you respond to a review, you are showing potential customers that you care enough to communicate with them. You also give Google the evidence it requires to rank you well in their search rankings. In my career, I've only seen reviews erased a handful of times, so the likelihood that the reviews and your responses will be around for a significant period of time is quite high. They are small assets that assist your business. Treat them with the respect they deserve and respond to reviews!

The impact of Google reviews is undeniable. We've seen meteoric jumps in rankings in Google Maps based on reviews alone. Yet, when we ask clients to get reviews, they will often ask folks once and then forget about it. The solution to getting reviews is to literally, step by step, show the review writer exactly what to do and where to go. Mobile phones are perfect for this. At Send It Rising, we've earned all of our reviews by asking "Would you mind writing a review for us?" in person. We then literally take their phone and navigate to where they need to go.

Granted, we have relatively few clients when you compare us to a restaurant or a handyman, so our reviews are harder to come by. However, we are only judged against those in our own industry. If you have a personal injury law firm, you only have to concern yourself with the number of reviews your competition has. If the typical review amount is 15, shoot for 30 reviews. You want your number of reviews to be dramatically higher than your nearest competitor, so that a potential customer doesn't have to spend much time thinking about which vendor to choose first.

Become comfortable asking for reviews on Google and Yelp. Remember that your Internet marketing team is handcuffed on earning you reviews, because they don't have the relationships that you do and people really need a strong push to write a 5-star review.

Simply adding "please review us" all over the Internet rarely creates satisfactory results. Respond to reviews and treat earning a review as a small sale with a tangible value.

Ask yourself today: what strategies can I implement to double my current reviews online? Where do I fall when measured against my competitors in this arena? Who could I ask for a review today?

Chapter Twenty-Four

ADVERTISE VS MONETIZE

Getting someone's attention is one thing. Making money from that attention through ads is an entirely different animal. Quantifying the value of a website visit is simple. The question I am more interested in is this: "Does the presence of the ad suck the soul from the site?" In this section, we look at making money, not from a product or service, but by showing ads for other companies on your website.

Recently ad blockers have become more prevalent online. As reported in NYtimes.com:

> ...one in five smartphone users, or almost 420 million people worldwide, (are) blocking advertising when browsing the web on cellphones.[14]

Let's look at a website that has no ads on it which generates 10,000 visits per month. Throwing some ads on the site through Google AdSense would generate approximately $50 a month, based on the average user. This won't pay the bills. However, it would provide the slightest amount of breathing room for the creator of the site to then dedicate more of their time to it, if he or she feels the site has the potential for them to earn a living. Is it possible that we can view the ads on the Internet as necessary byproducts required for certain sites to exist?

---

[14]   https://www.nytimes.com/2016/05/31/business/international/ smartphone-ad-blocking-software-mobile.html?_r=0

There is a term "banner blindness" that has shown that most people literally don't even see the ads. According to a study by Infolinks, "86% of consumers suffer from banner blindness."[15]

They literally spend next to no time at all looking at the ads because they've trained themselves to behave in that way. The obvious is that advertisers will become savvy to this and adapt.

Creating a website from nothing, paying the hosting fees, and spending an inordinate amount of time on it deserves some reward. If a company with a horrible reputation places an ad on your site through an online medium that you can't possibly police, is that just the cost of doing business? For most publishers online that is a simple yes.

---

[15]   http://neilpatel.com/blog/your-ads-are-getting-ignored-5-smart-strategies-to-overcome-banner-blindness/

Chapter Twenty-Five

LINK BUILDING

For years, link building referred to any link from a site outside of your own which points to your site. There was a time when we could trick Google's algorithm and have it believe that we were more important than we actually were, but those days are over.

Any attempt to try to manipulate search results through deception is foolhardy. We work with clients regardless of their past, which can come back to haunt them. For example, the 12,000 backlinks they purchased back in 2005 can suddenly send their rankings into the abyss.

Link building done right is this: create content relevant to your business and share it on social media platforms that Google recognizes and can be measured via Google Webmaster Tools. Remember Google and Facebook are competitors. Google Webmaster Tools, an absolute essential for anyone seriously interested in SEO, shows a detailed list of links that Google has found on the web that point to your site. In all of my years of doing this, I've never seen a link from Facebook. Not one. Does that tell you something? It should.

Matt Cutts, Google's former head of web spam, was interviewed and he, "made it clear that Google isn't always able to crawl all of the pages on Facebook and Twitter." [16]

---

[16]   https://www.stonetemple.com/
googles-matt-cutts-understanding-social-identity-on-the-web-is-hard/

It's no wonder we don't get to see those links in Google Webmaster Tools. Why would Facebook promote Google?

Your ability to provide evidence in the form of photos, videos and blogs will define your Internet presence and rankings in search engines. Give your employees the ability to promote your business through photos and videos. For example, we work with a garage door repair franchise with locations throughout California, and we've made it abundantly clear we would love photos and videos from them. They sent us a video, taken from a smartphone, of a garage door that had gone off its railing. The whole situation looked like a train wreck. Our client was called into fix the garage door, and the tech had been told by management that, should they run into something noteworthy, photos and videos would be appreciated. That video is up on YouTube, was embedded in the blog and shared via social media. The tech was also wise enough to take some pictures. All that media provides the evidence we need to not only rank well in Google but to create blog and social media content that is worth watching, liking and sharing.

Link building will continue to evolve. A nice way to visualize what link building looks like is to think of the neuro-network of your brain wherein every photo, word and video is a synapse. The more you create, the more interconnectivity you earn. It's no wonder that Google choose the words RankBrain to describe their AI algorithm.

The best strategy in this new environment is not to try to outwit this super-intelligent algorithm, rather it is to become the premier authority in your industry as evidenced by what we've shared on the Internet.

We've built tens of thousands of links from Pinterest by creating customized photos that have subsequently gone viral. Our best performing pin has over 20,000 repins. Because the photo in Pinterest links back to our website, each time it is repinned, we receive another link to our site.

Right this minute, make sure that you have Google Webmaster Tools installed on your site and check the links back to your site with regularity. When you create blog content, remember that you can build links from YouTube and Pinterest, and those links will appear in Google Webmaster Tools. And remember to take and share photos and videos!

Chapter Twenty-Six

ROBOTS

Using robots, you can follow thousands of new people across multiple Pinterest accounts daily. The same can be done on Twitter and Facebook. There is a tool called "iMacro," which can be added to Chrome or Firefox that allows you to program repeatable steps. You can even program time between steps. For instance, you might program the robot to follow someone on Pinterest every two minutes.

This begs the question, what are the ethics of using robots in advertising?

Let's say 25% of the people you follow on Pinterest will follow you back, and you follow 1,000 people per day. You'd earn 250 followers per day, and all 1,000 would receive a notification saying you now follow them, which is another form of advertising.

You could hire someone at $10 an hour to follow people all day, or you could have a robot do it. The frontier for robots in advertising is mind boggling. Now the majority of people using robots in marketing are spammers. They are fly-by-night companies which manipulate the web, and it's understandable why the major social media sites want to shut them down.

What could robots do in advertising? They could create and grow thousands of social media channels, interconnected to create a massive web of links and drive traffic to basically any site on the Internet. Imagine owning thousands of social media profiles, all with over 1,000 legitimate followers. If you want to promote something, you would then have a built-in audience.

We are going to see some very interesting Internet legislation occur in our lifetimes, and it will be fascinating to see the uninitiated try to wrap their heads around the automation that will drive businesses. If you can automate a machine to build a car, why can't you automate one to build a social profile?

If you are looking to grow a business, efficiency is necessary. The ethical lines are blurred when automation enters the picture. Is it ethical to have a program follow people on social media sites, in the hope that they will follow you back? This process has been defined as "Follow Churn" and is described as follows: "The practice of following someone just to get a follow back, and then un-following them." [17]

BlackHatWorld.com, the home of the Internet marketing dark side, has forums dedicated to the practice. (https://www.blackhatworld.com/seo/twitter-follow-unfollow-churn-limit.155022/)

Black hat Internet marketers are always testing the limits of what the social media sites will allow. Ultimately there is a dollar value associated with a follower, and if robots can earn followers, return on investment is possible.

Automation is not going to only take manufacturing jobs. It has already replaced jobs in Internet marketing. For example, many companies will automate their Facebook posts, auto-publishing a post once they've published a blog on Facebook. There are issues, of course, with automation of social media posts, which includes photos not showing up properly, links not working, and sentences being cut off before they naturally end.

Be conscious of not only whether you can use automation in your marketing through options like iMacro, but also where to draw the line.

---

[17]   http://www.urbandictionary.com/define.php?term=follow%20churn

Chapter Twenty-Seven

BREAKING DOWN
THE PSYCHE

Are you familiar with the term "breaking down and buying something?" This choice of words supposes that we are somehow broken should we choose to purchase something, which is an unfortunate way to look at a purchase. When we buy something, we often look at it as a loss of not only money but of will power. We weren't strong enough to resist the temptation. We "gave up" and "broke down" when we bought. This suggests guilt.

As businesspeople, we must be persistent and willing to have our egos bruised and be rejected. Depending on what you are selling, you will require a different number of touches before you can convert the prospect into a sale.

Here is a ballpark figure thrown out by BusinessInsider.com, "you have to contact the prospect a minimum of seven times within an 18-month period." [18]

Our natural inclinations as consumers towards avoiding buying something protects us against the endless stream of salespeople and marketers that see us as dollar signs instead of people. The multiple touches which sales people and organizations need to make before they close the sale naturally weeds out the businesses that don't

---

[18]   http://www.businessinsider.com/
how-many-contacts-does-it-take-before-someone-buys-your-product-2011-7

have the stamina to compete. The breaking down of a potential client through consistent advertising can also break down the advertiser, if they aren't careful. Advertising, especially Internet marketing, requires consistency to have an effect. Running a Facebook ad for a week and wondering why no sales comes in demonstrates a lack of understanding of how consumers shield themselves until a threshold is reached.

Trust is earned over time.

As you move forward with your business endeavors, keep in mind how a stream will eventually wear away a sharp rock into a smooth pebble. Keep your advertising budgets under control so that you can perpetually advertise, as opposed to starting and stopping. The effect of consistent advertising is cumulative, meaning that you are unlikely to see a lot of results up front. However over time the growth is often exponential, until you saturate your market. Hopefully you can repeat this process across regions and demographics once you understand the pace and patience required to advertise effectively without breaking down.

Chapter Twenty-Eight

TRIBES

The more speeches I give, the more I see how tribal people are. I recently spoke with a group of professionals in the insurance industry, and the consensus is that because the regulation on the industry is so strict and the potential liability so high, no one seems willing to take the risk of allowing their insurance agents access to what makes the Internet great, which is sharing.

These professionals agree that moving forward with blogging, creating videos and sharing online is the future, but no one seems willing to be the first one to take the risk. I love opportunities like this.

Because I am an outsider to the tribe, it's easy for me to call out the appropriate next step. The more difficult part is to convince one group to be the leader. I've seen the competitive nature of business play out where competitors fight for every inch of advantage. What's clear to me now is that there are often two or more battles waged simultaneously: the first in this case is against one another (simple capitalist competition), but the second is against a larger force (in this example the government, whose regulations threaten the entire tribe).

Politics aside, this dichotomy between the two parties galvanizes them. Both sides actively advertising to promote their vision. Where the insurance professionals fall short is in the lack of advertising created by individual agents, which could show the human side to their industry. It's easy for politicians to advertise their side of the story. They are, in fact, master advertisers -- if they're successful in politics at all.

As your company grows and you develop a sales force, remember that they have a vested interest in their personal brand and are looking for ways to reach new prospects. Limiting their ability to use social media effectively due to liability concerns can be shortsighted. Granted, there will always be mistakes that arise from allowing anyone to represent a brand. The fact that there might be a record of it online increases the potential threat.

That said, you should find ways to train your tribe on how to empower and grow their reputation. Invest in their education and lead by example. Every agent, as far as I am concerned, working for an insurance brokerage should have their own website and social media channels. Giving individuals one page on a corporate website is seriously limiting and demonstrates how much trust the organization places in their employees: not enough.

Chapter Twenty-Nine

DRAMA

Drama attracts us. To me, it feels like evolutionary software which tells us that drama may result in danger, so we need to pay attention. Drama is a multi-billion dollar industry and weaves its way into every facet of our lives, from our personal relationships to the office, to politics.

The Kardashians and Kris Jenner are the poster family for using drama to advertise themselves"

What we've seen since is a masterclass in controlling the media for one very specific gain: to keep viewers watching. I started to look at our careers like pieces on a chessboard," (Kris) Jenner wrote in her memoir. "Every day, I woke up and walked into my office and asked myself, 'What move do you need to make today?' It was very calculated. My business decisions and strategies were very intentional, definite and planned to the nth degree.[19]

People may complain about the drama, but that simply serves to reinforce the advertisement. To ignore drama completely... better yet, to leave the situation entirely is... the best remedy to any dramatic onslaught. Of course, this isn't always so easily done.

If you're engaged in some high-level, soul-sucking drama, know that those perpetuating it are paying the cost of their dramatic "advertising" in their own dignity. The more shameless the other, the

---

[19] https://www.buzzfeed.com/elliewoodward/how-the-kardashians-manipulated-the-media-to-become-the-most?utm_term=.exLBle45z#.riydZB6oP

more self-respect they are willing to sacrifice to pay the heavy cost of their manipulative campaign.

As in every ad run, unless the ads turn into sales, the ads stop (or should). This is how you eliminate drama from your life. Just change the channel on the dramatic ads. You can't engage them in any way, because every engagement is a buying sign. It leads the advertiser to believe that they may still make a sale. So, they keep bugging you. Just leave it alone, and they'll exhaust their emotional, dramatic budget.

There is a tremendous amount of power in simply ignoring something. An ad campaign that runs in which no one clicks or buys fizzles. Collectively we determine the future of the economy by determining what we choose to grant attention. In a more exaggerated form, we shape the future by what we buy.

However, you must understand that simply visiting a website is a kind of purchase if that website earns revenue from banner ads. It isn't enough to say, "I've never purchased from XYZ company." If you comment on their Facebook page, or even speak against them in public, you're advertising for them.

For example, leaving a one star review for a local restaurant can actually help them rank higher. The content, which is typically long-form, in negative reviews is picked up by search engines. The owners of the restaurant typically respond, and the end result is that the restaurant ranks higher and can actually come across as more authentic, given that all of their reviews don't appear "fake."

Put simply, if you are against something or someone, consider the power of ignoring them and their advertisements. If you must engage, keep it short. If we collectively ignore companies, or groups of people, we can minimize their return on investment of time, energy and dollars.

I've seen countless groups railing against organizations, which only provides them with more publicity. This can even make the organization they hate seem much larger and more powerful than it is. Consider putting your energy toward something positive which you control: your social media or website. Attention is currency. Don't waste it.

Chapter Thirty

MIND YOUR OWN BUSINESS

That's a very strange saying: "Mind your own business." It implies that you are paying attention to something private, but the words themselves reveal part of our collective consciousness as English speakers. We consider business to be private. And more and more, we see that our businesses are anything but private.

Where advertisements used to be confined to word of mouth, the radio, and 30 second television clips, ads now include scathing online reviews, people who make fun of you on your YouTube Channel, and sites that crop up criticizing your business for perceived improprieties.

I love it. What an amazing time to be alive.

If we as a community finally have the power to call out business, either positively or negatively, I feel as though we not only have the right, but the obligation to do so. If something bad happens at a business, isn't it our responsibility to help other patrons avoid that same problem? Responsibility and justice run hand in hand. Businesses that take responsibility, own up to their shortcomings and work to better themselves are just like the people who do the same things in their personal lives. We call them mature adults.

So, this old concept of "mind your own business" is dying quickly. There is no minding your own business anymore. Millions of others and I are going to mind your business as well as our own. We're going to write about what we think, and we know our reviews carry the weight that they should. "90% of consumers read online reviews before visiting a business. And 88% of consumers trust online reviews as much as personal recommendations." [20]

That noted, there are crazy, ridiculous people on this planet. And if one of these folks takes it upon him or herself to slander a business online in the form of a scathing review, the only responsible recourse as a business owner is to respond in a mature and dignified manner. Good luck with the crazy, ridiculous people by the way.

But before you get too depressed, know that one bad review out of 20 or more reviews doesn't show that your business is bad. It demonstrates that some people are crazy, and it can actually lend credibility to your business because it shows that your reviews, at least some of them, are legitimate.

Don't forget that if someone goes to a review site of yours and sees a one star review, they are still on your site. Every moment is one more in which they are on a page you own. That's advertising time which you are earning through having a bad review. And if that bad review is nestled among many, many positive ones, and you've responded to the negative review reasonably, you can turn even the worst review into advertising gold.

20   http://www.invespcro.com/blog/the-importance-of-online-customer-reviews-infographic/

Chapter Thirty-One

THE BODY'S ADS

You've been in pain: the kind that refuses to let you sleep and won't let you focus. Pain is terrible, and it draws your attention better than anything else, because at the end of the day your body is your company, your future, your everything.

The problem with the advertising that your body does, is that it doesn't come with a solution. Nerves just yell at you, "Something is wrong!" over and over again. This form of advertising is incredibly persuasive, because you can't do anything until you somehow manage to figure out what it is that went wrong. And until then, it's as if nothing else matters.

The body is so effective at this form of advertising that we've created a multi-billion dollar pharmaceutical industry that specializes in blocking these pain advertisements our nerves send us. TrinityOrthopedics.com writes:

> In recent years, a variety of studies have examined different age groups experiencing chronic pain, comparing the effects of the pain and assessing how memory and concentration are impaired. A study done in Alberta, Canada, suggests that pain disrupts the body's maintenance of the memory trace that is essential in holding information for processing and retention. Participants found their pain so distracting that they

could not focus, which in turn impaired their memories during the period of the study. [21]

Your organization can undergo immense pain by way of the overall health of the business, but also pain felt by individuals within the company. Small companies are vulnerable to the effects of a single team member's suffering. Businesses in many ways are like a body. Even if only your little finger hurts, the entire system can lose focus. Masking the pain is not a good long term solution. Quickly addressing the issue and taking steps to prevent it recurring is the best path forward.

Recognize the lack of concentration that can ripple across a business when anyone in the company is hurting. This applies not only to physical pain, but emotional and psychological pain too. An ideal company invests in the well-being of all team members and doesn't shy away from, or attempt to deaden, pain points. Instead, an excellent company recognizes and immediately takes steps to identify the source of the pain and looks to heal as soon as possible.

---

[21] http://www.trinityorthopedics.com/chronic-pain-concentration/

Chapter Thirty-Two

HOW TO SPEAK ADVERTISING

You've seen that most human interaction can be summed up as advertising, that our intrinsic need for attention is at the core of what we hold dear. You've also considered the numerous ways in which we advertise. So, how do we speak the language of advertising fluently, and how do we profit from it?

We live in the early artificial intelligence age, and everything we communicate online is judged, not only by other people, but also by the growing super-intelligence currently operated by Alphabet (Google).

Without our voices resonating online, we are in trouble. Bringing our expertise to the Internet is a requirement for business in this new era.

Some people don't want a lot of attention. The camera isn't their friend, and they have no interest in fame. Feeling uncomfortable with a great deal of attention isn't something that fades when you graduate high school. For most it lasts a lifetime. As adults, we can avoid things we don't want to do, especially public speaking.

Test yourself. You can begin by drawing attention in your personal life. See how long you can hold the attention of those around you without becoming obnoxious. Ask questions. Remember, listening is a great way of earning someone's attention. Back and forth is a prerequisite to hold attention.

If you are going to make a request for someone's attention, be sure you are willing to stop and listen where appropriate. Politicians know that they can only hold attention for a certain period of time. Hollywood knows it. Movies rarely exceed three hours. Pop songwriters of every genre know it, typically not going past five minutes for their big hits. Knowing how long you can hold an individual's attention easily translates into how long you can hold an audience's attention. Practice for an audience of one, first, whether literally or in your mind's eye.

One of the main reasons people want to pay attention to you is because you are an authority. The moment you show impatience or that you are irritated they aren't paying attention, you admit your content isn't engaging enough to keep their attention and that they should pay attention to you simply because you are speaking.

There are limitless ways to speak advertising. Digital is a metrics-based game in which we can measure engagement. Time on site, click through rate, bounce rate, and return visitation are all clues as to how much attention we've earned. These metrics can be endlessly analyzed to provide insight into the direction to move in the future. Don't get too caught up in analytics however, as it can easily become something that you focus on entirely, missing opportunities to act and continue to advertise.

You can write "advertising" as a language just as you can speak it. Embedding videos onto a site's blog is great, but the page should also contain the written word. Most people skim blogs. No one reads every word of every page they see on the Internet. With that in mind, include headers in your content that are engaging, shocking, and/or blunt. Know that most people are just going to read the headers and skim a few lines. If you can lock them in with the headers, you can get them to spend more time on the page, increasing your impact.

Obviously, this book is an example of written advertising, in which every section is designed to hold your attention and draw you into the next chapter.

By actively practicing the language of advertising at your job and in your entrepreneurial efforts, you will become more and more fluent, learning how to earn and hold attention for longer periods of time. If the attention you earn is strong enough, you can convert that into action.

Let's also look at something most of us can relate to -- relationships. To get married, you have to sell someone on the idea that they should spend the rest of their life with you. Whether that actually happens is beside the point and the subject of many books on keeping a healthy marriage. To convince someone to spend the rest of their life with you requires a fluency in advertising. Every date is a planned event, requiring forethought and consistent communication. It's easy to see parallels between business and dating. Keeping top of mind is a core component of advertising effectively. In a relationship, a great deal of time is spent earning and sharing attention.

The goal is to learn how to broaden that experience to a larger number of people. Know that the advertising you've practiced in your relationships relates to the attention you seek from large audiences. You just need to apply those principles to a greater number of people. Politicians create fanatics who are practically in love with, or avidly hate, them. This is simply an extension of our relationship mentality. We can't help but feel this way or that way about the people whom we know. Becoming known is the key.

SECTION THREE

IT'S PERSONAL

I met James (not his actual name) at a country club in Las Vegas where I gave a speech about adapting to the evolving Internet landscape. We chatted after my speech, and he invited me to connect with a local hotel and casino here in Las Vegas. I accepted.

Turns out James is an old-school sales guy with some interesting techniques. You see, he will just walk into the backend of a major business and somehow, someway get in front of a decision maker and book a meeting.

He says, "I never lie. If you get caught in a lie, it's over."

So, when people ask him if he has a meeting with the person he's trying to get in touch with, he will respond "No, I am looking to get on their calendar." Then he asks for help.

"People," he says, "nine times out of ten are happy to help. What's the worst they can do? Kick you out?"

This old-school style fascinates me, especially given how focused I am on Internet marketing and leveraging modern technology to advertise. His style reminds me that the old-school sales game is alive and well. He's proof. In many ways, his form of advertising, given that it's been honed for decades, is similar to Internet marketing. He can enter a space and walk out with a meeting.

On our journey, he closed some business with a contact he'd had from a previous sale. What's so fascinating about his technique is that he can advertise, convert, and advertise again in a matter of seconds. A conversion for him may simply be to acquire the name of the person he wants to meet, or it might be to receive an introduction to the person who knows the person that he's seeking. This all happens in a matter of minutes.

Once he's in, what most would consider the "real advertising" begins. This is the 30 second elevator pitch. The mini-conversions that occur along the way result only in the opportunity to advertise to the decision maker.

He tells me that a previous employer of his once said, "If you leave one more voicemail, I am going to fire you."

No one responds to sales voicemails and to his thinking, it makes much more sense to simply walk through those "Employee Only" doors and get to work than to just be another sales guy bothering people with cold calls. I admire the guts it takes to do that. James earns his money.

Chapter Thirty-Three

BOARD OR BORED?

Dr. Victoria Boyd has a trajectory that fascinates me. I called her out of the blue one day, and luckily, she picked up. Since then, I've been a speaker with her IMPACT Learning Conference, and she's introduced me to her concept of Philantrepreneurship.

Merging philanthropy with entrepreneurship is where I would love to see marketing go, by which the philanthropy of a company becomes its marketing. This concept is often referred to as cause marketing. Cause marketing aligns a brand with a cause in the community. This can help kids learn to read or feed the homeless. When managed well, cause marketing can have a measurable impact on the business and builds goodwill and loyalty among the customer base.

According to a national survey by Cone Communications, 87% of consumers say they would switch from one brand to another if the other brand were associated with a good cause. [22]

When I was younger, a seat on a board conjured up images of men smoking cigars in suits as they debate the future of their enterprise. Now that I've been invited to sit on the board of directors for the Philantrepreneur Foundation, I see a much different and better image. Teaching nonprofits how to think like a business can be a challenge. My friend Dr. Boyd's brain-child, the Philantrepreneur Foundation, does just that by educating, consulting and improving nonprofits. The foundation is the nonprofit for nonprofits. It's also

---

[22]   https://www.entrepreneur.com/article/197820

now an ally for Send It Rising's cause marketing campaigns and has introduced my business to countless nonprofits.

As a marketer, I can tell you that the nonprofits with which I've spoken often have a strong sense of purpose, ample desire, but little to no technical experience. From web development to SEO, Pay Per Click to Analytics, they often don't have the data or expertise to manage a strategic digital marketing campaign across multiple channels. Now, they know that digital marketing is important, but would rather focus on what brought them to their nonprofit in the first place -- helping. Unfortunately, the online infrastructure is in many ways a predecessor to the charity. For those of you reading this who are involved with, or are considering creating a nonprofit, here are some startup tips to get the ball rolling.

1. While you are developing your website, roll out your social media platforms and begin to build them.
2. Once the site is live and optimized, you are going to have to be creating a consistent stream of content through the blog. Be prepared to invest time into this.
3. Take pictures and videos of everything. A behind the scenes look into a nonprofit is much more interesting than you might think.
4. Identify keywords for which you'd like to appear in Google and measure them. Download software that tracks search engine rankings across keywords.
5. Install Google Analytics and Google Webmaster Tools on your website.
6. Experiment with small Facebook ad budgets and measure what works.
7. Play with small YouTube Ad budgets and hone in on the videos that are getting the best traction.

If you find yourself in the nonprofit space, think like a business. Getting donations is much like selling. Create social media that is compelling, and understand that you may have to spend money to make money. This is just part of the way the world works! Keep the entrepreneurial spirit alive, even if you find yourself in a nonprofit.

Chapter Thirty-Four

PLANET HOLLYWOOD

Even though I've lived in Las Vegas for years, the Strip still has a magical quality to it. As I was driving to my first paid speaking engagement at Planet Hollywood, I was struck by how far I'd come from my little hometown in North Dakota. Public speaking is often listed as one of people's biggest fears, and that is understandable. If I hadn't taught school first, it's possible that I never would have gotten into public speaking at all.

I spoke at DepoSpan, which is a conference for court reporters around the nation. I always get to these events early to meet people and then use what I've learned in the speech for that day. Once I was introduced, I had the option to either use the microphone or simply speak loudly to this room of 50+ people. That teaching experience came in handy. I simply raised my voice, made sure everyone could hear me clearly and kept going.

It would seem as though a speaking engagement like this one doesn't have much of a digital component, so I made sure that we added one. The speech was filmed, and as part of the presentation I invited a few people down to chat in front of the camera to show how easy it is to make a YouTube video.

If you ever make it on stage to speak in front of a group, please do yourself the favor of taking photo and video. Rick 'Siloh' Moses, founder of WeWin360!, was awarded a Certificate of Special Congressional Recognition for an unwavering commitment and leadership to help the disadvantaged people of Las Vegas for his work with #ServingHopeLV. He spoke at the NonProfit Awareness Expo, and I attended his speech. He got a standing ovation, and it wasn't caught on film or with pictures. When invited to speak, make absolutely sureyou are ready to capture the moment.

Chapter Thirty-Five

BILLBOARDS & CREDIBILITY

"How much?" I said, in disbelief. I was under the impression that billboards were expensive. I'd heard 11k thrown around in casual conversation, so it might just be great timing, but we secured a deal for a lot less than that. As a busy business owner, I don't always know what I am walking into. This particular morning, I called my colleague and asked her to please look up the name of the person I was going to be introduced to as I rushed to the meeting. It turns out this professional was a salesperson for a new, digital billboard company actively searching for clients.

When we were told how much it would cost to get onto a billboard, we were shocked. They made it abundantly clear that our wholesale rate was to be kept confidential, so I won't mention it here. Suffice it to say, we have both SendItRising.com and KellenKautzman.com on billboards. The credibility alone was enough for us to want to pull the trigger.

We now also offer billboards to our clients for reasonable prices and make a dollar or two in the process. Advertising is all about relationships.

I look at these digital billboards as extensions of my computer screen. They are very much an Internet marketing push because we are able to measure site visits that come from them. Our new partner mentioned that they almost always choose to put the website up over the phone number, because no one seems to call billboards with phone numbers anymore. At face value, I can see why people wouldn't consider billboards Internet marketing. However, I can now gain close to one million impressions a month by creating images on my computer and sending it to our new partner to add to our digital billboards. That's a good feeling.

Let's remember the considerable difference between an old, physical billboard and a new digital one. Digital billboards allow for creative flexibility and require no printing. No wonder the price is reasonable. Our billboard partner made a wonderful point when she said, "You can change the message every day." If it's Monday, you can switch up the wording. If it's a holiday, you can simply create a new billboard that reflects the day. It's truly incredible how digital billboards allow for creativity to be unleashed and altered based on what's working and what isn't, much like a website.

Chapter Thirty-Six

ADVERTISING TO YOUR TEAM

Your team is vitally important to your success. A colleague of mine, one of my key team members, when asked "How is your workload?" usually responds with, "I have a solid eight hours a day." I believe her!

When I asked her today, "Did you complete XYZ task?" she had a look on her face that I know very well. It is the look of "I have been working every millisecond of this day and that task did not make my priority list." We both laughed because we're both fighting tooth and nail for the success of this company, and we're both in the trenches with our hands dirty, which brings me to my point: advertising internally is a critical component in the success of any company. As a leader, you must show interest in the work of your team. As Dale Carnegie put it, "You can make more friends in two months by becoming interested in other people than you can in two years by trying to get other people interested in you."

Working hard is difficult enough, and if you want a successful company there will be plenty of that! But working hard with no appreciation is almost unbearable. There an article by Tony Schwartz in the Harvard Business Review called "Why Appreciation Matters So Much" in which Mr. Schwartz writes:

> The single highest driver of engagement, according to a worldwide study conducted by Towers Watson, is whether

or not workers feel their managers are genuinely interested in their wellbeing. Less than 40 percent of workers felt so engaged.[23]

Appreciation advertising requires effort from management. And there is a significant difference between genuine appreciation and lip service. Flattering a team member by saying, "Nice job!" when you aren't sure if they did a good job can come across as you not appreciating what they've done. To really be genuine requires an investment of time to understand the work of your team and to earn their attention via advertisements that show that you know what they've done. Be lavish in your praise! This appreciation advertising will return strongly on your time investment. We all know that to work with someone who truly appreciates us makes all the difference.

---

[23]   https://hbr.org/2012/01/why-appreciation-matters-so-mu

Chapter Thirty-Seven

EMAIL LISTS & GOLF

Attempting to hit the ball out of the sand trap repeatedly and failing miserably seems to have very little to do with email lists. I was golfing at Legacy here in Las Vegas with a few business associates, and for those of you who play this tragically difficult game, you'll know that patience is the primary golf virtue. Golf has long been an excellent way to spend a few hours with others.

In this outing, I didn't play well (but then I never do), but I remained patient under pressure. We all did. By all accounts it was a successful 18 holes. Toward the end, making small talk with a friend, I mentioned an event that we'd intended to host through the Philantrepreneur Foundation. My friend, being a member of multiple chambers of commerce around Las Vegas offered to allow us to use the chambers email lists. Our reach went from a few hundred to a few thousand in an instant.

Missing the golf ball in a sand trap doesn't seem like it will lead to an exponentially larger email database, but then again, you never know the extent to which friends can help you until you ask.

Be good to people and be patient.

Chapter Thirty-Eight

$1,500,000

This is the price tag of a stunning home I just toured. Getting roped into random meetings has become a semi-regular occurrence, and today's meeting was no different. I'd chatted with a real estate agent who was going to introduce me to a friend of his. We met at a local coffee joint and they invited me to their next meeting. Turns out the meeting is for a 1.5 million dollar property that is unlike any I've ever seen. There is a pool, spa and waterfall in the center of the home, and all the rooms connect to that main pool area. There is industrial equipment that runs this home, which is fully automated. The couple attempting to sell the home are in their 80's and would like to move. They've gone with multiple realtors, each of whom has failed.

Why? Marketing.

Marketing a home like this presents unique challenges. The pool, which actually doesn't use chlorine to clean it, gives off a lot of humidity. There is an industrial dehumidifier in the garage for that purpose. There are "Star Trek" doors to the master bedroom, a well on the property and all the maintenance costs of owning an indoor pool. The guidebook for the home is biblically large.

This home goes to show that expertise in marketing is a key component to any successful business. The "carrot on the stick" as the homeowner put it "is $50,000." There is a significant chunk of change lying in wait for the real estate team savvy enough to market this stunning home.

Chapter Thirty-Nine

MILLENNIAL CONGRESSMEN

I received an email from the Innevation Center asking if I'd be interested in chatting with some congressmen in a roundtable as the representatives were looking for millennial minds to discuss technology. The roundtable consisted of 10 members. The three congressmen were Darren Soto (theU.S. Representative forFlorida's 9th district), Ruben Kihuen (U.S. Representative for Nevada's 4th congressional district,) and Eric Swalwell (U.S. Representative from California's 15th congressional district).

My two cents in the hour and a half conversation included the need to include cause marketing as a way for businesses of all sizes to take responsibility for their communities through engaging with nonprofits. The position of cause marketer will also provide a new set of jobs in the Internet economy.

Automation is coming, and we're going to need to find meaningful work for those that have lost their employment. If we can prove there is a positive return on investment for businesses with heart, those which go into the community, do good work, support charities and share their efforts via social media, we can create a huge number of jobs. Small businesses are the heart and muscle of the American economy.

According to sba.gov:

> The 28 million small businesses in America account for 54% of all U.S. sales. Small businesses provide 55% of all jobs and 66% of all net new jobs since the 1970s.

> The 600,000 plus franchised small businesses in the
> U.S. account for 40% of all retail sales and provide jobs
> for some 8 million people. The small business sector in
> America occupies 30-50% of all commercial space, an
> estimated 20-34 billion square feet. [24]

Now imagine how widespread a cause marketing focus could be when adopted by small businesses across the United States. This adoption would invigorate the economy because it would provide jobs and stimulate the nonprofit sector, potentially lowering crime and raising the standard of living for those of us who need it most. A nationwide shift in thinking from typical marketing to cause marketing would have a profound effect on the economy, number of jobs, job satisfaction, and effectiveness of grassroots nonprofits.

---

[24]   https://www.sba.gov/managing-business/running-business/
energy-efficiency/sustainable-business-practices/small-business-trends

Chapter Forty

HATERS INC.

If you are doing anything worth doing, you will find a small, vocal segment of the population who are interested in humiliating you. The comment section can be a ruthless expression of our First Amendment rights.

Once you reach a certain level of popularity, the haters will appear. Ironically, they are an important element of the Internet ecosystem, because they gather attention.

Let's take a look at a hater on YouTube. Google's algorithms, including that of YouTube, read every word on practically every page. When a troll shows up on your YouTube video and decides this is an opportune place to dump their garbage, it would be wise to reflect on the SEO benefit of their waste disposal.

You see, the additional content helps your video rank well in YouTube search. It also shows activity on the video and may inspire more comments. Haters, especially on YouTube, actually work for you by spending precious time as a writer for your company. Granted, what they say may be offensive, rude or simply cruel, but what can you expect from free labor? They are working on behalf of your enterprise, gratis. The only appropriate thing to do is thank them for their feedback. After all, you are the beneficiary. If your gratitude encourages more outrage, excellent!

Don't let the fear of the opinions of others stop you from pursuing and sharing your message with the world. As an entrepreneur or business owner, you are ultimately fending for yourself, family and community. If there are those out there that would wish you mere verbal harm, chalk it up to jealousy or something that simply has next to nothing to do with you.

Once the haters show up, take it as a sign that you are onto something. Their growth will parallel your ascent in your increasingly successful career.

CONCLUSION

The word "advertise" comes from the Latin "advertere," which means "to turn toward." Anything you do that causes someone to look at, listen, or consider you is an advertisement. SEO, pay per click, website development and social media are all simply modern day outlets for you to advertise. Luckily, you've been advertising your entire life. From cradle to grave, we reach out for people's attention and those of us that master it wield incredible power, not only financially, but in our relationships as well. Seriously consider where you pay the most attention as it carries tremendous weight.

With the rise of artificial intelligence, we know that evidence online is key. Continue to create content and prove that you are an authority by the consistent production of videos, blogs and photos shared on your site and then through the appropriate social media channels.

When looking to rank well in search engines, know that you are entering a competition with others that are striving for those same high rankings. Treat this endeavor just as you would a tournament. To rank well requires grit, tenacity and determination. This is an ongoing battle. How long it will take you to get there is anyone's guess.

No organization that you hire can do what you can. As the business owner, founder, or entrepreneur your relationships with your clients have a direct impact on the business. Take behind the scenes pictures. Get in front of the camera. Ask your clients for reviews.

Remember that you were a kid once and taking business seriously all the time can lead to stagnation, especially in your advertising. Learning how to become light hearted in itself can be a phenomenal advertisement. Laugh, love, smile.

Don't shy away from sharing painful experiences that have lead you to where you are now. Many celebrities become famous through sharing what they've gone through. This, of course, requires sharing at the appropriate time and place. That being said, the weight of being real with your audience makes for excellent ads.

If a client of yours has a story that is impactful, ask for their permission to share it. They may become a raving fan and help you share the story as well. This goes beyond simple testimonials and into authentic sharing that has the potential to go viral.

Pursue media opportunities wherever they may lie. From RadioGuestList.com to local TV shows and podcasts, actively pursue authority in your industry through appearances on shows. At the very least, you will get a link to your website from it.

Do not, under any circumstances, hire a company to build links for you without your supervision. You need to know what links are pointing to your site and ensure that they are white hat, ethical and authoritative.

With your loved ones, friends and family, realize that you are also advertising. If you are struggling to "make a sale" and get your way, reconsider what your ads look like. Are they entertaining, interesting and appealing? Are they repetitive, boring and predictable?

Pay attention to the thoughts that you allow into your mind. Are you actively advertising your goals and positivity, or are you letting a barrage of negative thoughts enter into the equation? In many ways, you are responsible for the habits that occur from the thoughts you allow into your mind. Just like in business, this will determine your future success or failure.

Getting the most attention isn't always the best move. As in the world of sports, telegraphing, or overtly showing your intention, can work against you. Be conscious of the situations that require subtlety.

Growing your own celebrity is entirely feasible within your location and field of expertise. Videos are a simple and effective way to do just that. You may never be world famous, but you can carve out a niche that makes you wealthy within your community.

Just like the world's greatest musicians, you are an entertainer. Your social media channels, blogs and videos are all an avenue through which you can hold people's attention and get them excited about your product or service. Don't be afraid to tell a joke, let loose and entertain!

Babies are excellent advertisers. They cry and they get all of their needs met. Yet, when they grow older, those ads no longer work as well as they used to. Our businesses need to adapt as they grow and age.

If you find yourself at the top of an organization, empower those beneath you to join the marketing team. Give them the ability to take photos and videos and submit them to the marketing department. Everyone should be involved in the marketing of the company.

If a company has ample online reviews, they will see more business. Yet, receiving positive reviews takes a considerable effort. Consider getting an online review like making a sale. Invest in it.

As you earn more and more attention, remember that you still are running a business and you have to ask for the sale. Some businesses struggle with the right combination of education, entertainment and commercials. Continue to experiment until you find the right blend for your business.

Find time once a week to create videos and share them on YouTube. Embed the YouTube video on your blog and share that via social media. Advertise your YouTube videos through AdWords in your local area. Become a local celebrity.

Keep your head up! This is a lot of work and remaining optimistic is going to help you make your way through it. Optimism not only helps you stay focused, it will help keep your team motivated and on point.

There is a tremendous opportunity in learning how to leverage automation to help grow your Internet marketing campaigns. IMacro is one example of simple programming that will allow you to automate some of the processes that you could easily spend through hiring someone.

Persistence is key. When looking at your advertising budget, keep in mind that one year may be necessary to see the results you are looking for. Many potential customers require multiple touches before they'll consider purchasing from your business.

Meet people from various organizations that gather around a mutual interest. Be bold. Find ways to enter into these spaces and tailor your message to meet their interests.

Spark the fire of the motivational speaker within you! Not everyone wants the details, or to be taught. Many folks want you to get them energized and excited about making a substantial change in their life. Fill them with an abundance of energy and watch the magic happen.

Drama is inevitable and can easily drain the energy from your organization. Don't feed the fire. Drama is an ad campaign and needs sales to continue. Learn how to extinguish the blaze by not providing it the oxygen it desires.

Everyone is going to mind your business. You can turn this to your advantage by encouraging them to do so. Respond to reviews, positive and negative. If someone leaves a nasty comment, thank them for their feedback. The more time they spend interacting with your brand the better.

Just as your body will let you know if there is something wrong through pain, your company will experience similar stress and frustration. Pain is simply an indicator that something needs to change. Stress, angry customers and frustration are all ways of your business telling you that you need to shift.

Combine your old-school techniques with new technology to leverage the benefits from both worlds.

Seriously consider aligning with a nonprofit for mutual benefit and to make the world a better place. If you are currently on the board of a nonprofit, treat it like a business!

If you find yourself speaking in front of a group of people, take ample photos and record video. You'll be glad you did.

Rare advertising deals may present themselves to you. Keep an eye out for these amazing opportunities. Don't let your preconceived notion of the price stop you from investigating.

Your team is everything. Make them feel special and advertise your appreciation for their work both publicly and privately.

Just because it doesn't look like an Internet marketing opportunity, doesn't mean it isn't one. Everyone now has access to social media profiles, websites and email lists that you could use by establishing the right relationship with them.

There is tremendous compensation waiting for those with the appropriate marketing skill and determination.

Being an excellent advertiser can get you in front of powerful people. Knowing what to do with their attention can rocket you to the top.

Haters aren't going to disappear anytime soon. You'll need a thick skin to play at a high level. Remember that they are helping you advertise for free. Thank them and move on.

By now you are an expert in understanding advertising. You can see that nearly any interaction can be understood in the context of an ad. Embrace the Internet and all the advertising opportunities with your newfound understanding. Realize that every possible new technology is only an avenue through which you are able to advertise your business. There is no moment that goes without an advertisement.

Now is your time to shine, knowing that you are capable of greatness through courage and consistently advertising your desires in effective and entertaining ways. Become a celebrity in your space. Advertise in every moment.

ABOUT THE AUTHOR

Kellen owns Send It Rising Internet Marketing and manages a team of over 20 internet marketing professionals. He was the keynote speaker at Planet Hollywood on the Las Vegas strip and has spoken at Roseman University and the Lance Tamashiro podcast. Kellen holds a master's degree in education and taught for five years before transitioning into his career as an internet marketer. Kellen speaks fluent Spanish and has a family with his wife Lonaeja, daughter Anika and son Phoenix.

www.ingramcontent.com/pod-product-compliance
Lightning Source LLC
Chambersburg PA
CBHW051707170526
45167CB00002B/573